D0580459

FRANK LLOYD WRIGHT

A STUDY IN ARCHITECTURAL CONTENT

FRANK LLOYD WRIGHT
A STUDY IN ARCHITECTURAL CONTENT

Norris Kelly Smith

AMERICAN LIFE FOUNDATION & STUDY INSTITUTE

Published by The American Life Foundation in

The Institute for the Study of Universal History Through Arts and Artifacts series

Modern History in the Arts

The first edition of *Frank Lloyd Wright: A Study in Architectural Content* was published by Prentice-Hall, Inc. in 1966. Since then the book has been out-of-print and Prentice-Hall Inc. assigned the copyright to the author. This edition has been revised by the author, re-designed, re-set, and some new illustrations added. Any inquiries about the book should be directed to: Professor Norris Kelly Smith, Department of Art and Archaeology, Washington University, St. Louis, Missouri, 63130.

© 1979 Norris Kelly Smith

ISBN: 0-89257-006-7

The author wishes to thank Horizon Press Publishers Ltd., New York for permission to quote from *The Future of Architecture* by Frank Lloyd Wright, copyright © 1953, and for permission to use the photographs of Taliesen at Spring Green, Wisconsin from *An American Architecture* by Frank Lloyd Wright, © 1960. The publisher wishes to thank Horizon Press Publishers Ltd., for permission to use drawings of the exterior and interior of the Larkin Building and the Preliminary Design for the Coonley House from *An American Architecture* by Frank Lloyd Wright copyright © 1960.

All color plates and new illustrations © copyright, Thomas A. Heinz, P.O Box 663, Oak Park, IL 60303. Information about The Frank Lloyd Wright Association ("a forum for the study of America's foremost architect" with its beautiful quarterly *Newsletter*) can be had from PO Box 2100, Oak Park, IL 60303.

All rights reserved. No part of this book may be reproduced in any form or by any means without permission in writing from the publishers: The American Life Foundation, Box 349, Watkins Glen, NY, 14891 607-535-4737

Production notes: Design and Production by Walnut Grove Associates, Watkins Glen, NY. Composition in Linotype Baskerville, Goudy Titling, Goudy Oldstyle, and Palatino Italic by Tier Oldstyle Typesetting, Binghamton, NY. Color separations by Callahan Color Service, Binghamton, NY. Printing by Valley Offset, Inc., Deposit, NY. The paperback was bound by Valley Offset. Inc. The hardcover edition was bound by Publisher's Book Bindery. Finch Opaque Smooth in a seventy-pound weight was used for the text. Mead Black and White Enamel in an eighty-pound weight was used for the plates which were printed in 200-line screen. This edition is two thousand paper and one thousand casebound.

In gratitude, to

Meyer Shapiro

Table of Contents

PROLOGUE

BUT WHERE WILL YOU BE WHEN AMERICA GETS around to all this? Do you expect to live a hundred years longer?"[1] So spoke Kuno Francke in 1908 when he visited Frank Lloyd Wright at his home in Oak Park and tried to persuade him to come to Germany, where people were ready and waiting, he thought, for what the American architect was doing. We have here, it would seem, the first explicit statement of two ideas that have for the most part dominated the study and criticism of Wright's work for the past forty or fifty years: the first, that he was "ahead of his time," a pioneer whose vision of the future was beyond the ken of his contemporaries in Chicago, bemused as they were with historical styles and with recollections of their Columbian Exposition; and the second, that Europe was advancing in the same direction as he, so that when he fled to Germany in 1909, he carried thither the seminal ideas that were to bring forth in Germany and the Netherlands a flowering of modern architecture that should rightly have occurred in Chicago. It has seemed important, that is, to link Wright securely with the Modern Movement—to justify or authenticate his work on the basis of its relationship to the continuing development of modern design. As Nikolaus Pevsner put it in 1936, "[Wright's] position in 1903 was almost identical with that of the most advanced thinkers on the future of art and architecture today."[2]

It becomes increasingly clear that we have been less concerned with Wright than with his place in the history—or, better, the legendary saga—of modern architecture. Our thinking has been shaped mainly by certain still widely cherished presuppositions about the relation of architecture to its "times." Each age, we have long been taught to believe, has brought forth an architecture expressing its own spirit or character. Or at least this was the normal order of things until the nineteenth century, at which time the processes of social change, accelerated by political and industrial revolution, outstripped the professional architect and left him behind, out of touch with the new cul-

1. Frank Lloyd Wright, *An Autobiography,* 2nd ed. (New York: Duell, Sloane, and Pearce, 1943), p. 162.

2. Nikolaus Pevsner, *Pioneers of Modern Design from William Morris to Walter Gropius* (New York: Museum of Modern Art, 1949), p. 34.

ture and able to speak only the dead languages of extinct civilizations. Yet the new spirit inevitably found expression—at first in the unselfconscious and almost anonymous works of structural engineers such as Telford and Brunel, later in the inventions of a generation of young architects, among them Wagner, Voysey, Mackintosh, Perret, and Sullivan, who rejected the dead styles and experimented boldly with the new materials, new techniques of construction, and new architectural occasions of the technological civilization that was being born. And so from their work there has evolved a rational and efficient modern style which is as much in keeping with the scientific and pragmatic spirit of our era as was the aspiring Gothic with that of the Age of Faith.

The argument seems plausible enough. Our world today is more evidently shaped by works of science and industry than was the Gothic world by works of Christian faith. Yet one would think it might give the architect pause to observe that neither painters nor poets nor musicians have been inclined to concur in his assessment of the twentieth century. To them it has seemed, more often than not, an age of anxiety and despair, of unreason and absurdity, of meaninglessness and alienation. They have produced works in an astonishing variety of styles, almost none of which shows an affinity with the scientific or technological aspects of our civilization. Whether we may better characterize our era in Walter Gropius's terms or in John Cage's is hard to say—so hard, in fact, that we have cause to wonder if living artists have ever been able to know the nature of their "age," or if it is worth our while to think in such terms at all.

Yet it cannot be denied that an important part in the shaping of modern architecture has been played by the idea, fostered by modern historicism, that the culture of every society is internally consistent and homogeneous. As Louis Sullivan expressed it, "At no time and in no instance has [architecture] been other than an index of the flow of the thought of the people—an emanation from the inmost life of the people. . . . For as a people thinks concerning Architecture, so it thinks concerning everything else; and as it thinks concerning any other thing, so it thinks concerning Architecture; for the thought of a people, however complicated it may appear, is all of-a-piece." [3] But

3. Louis Sullivan, "What Is Architecture: A Study in the American People Today," *American Contractor,* XXVII (January 1906), 49.

of course if this were true, how could Sullivan's own thought have been so at variance with that of his contemporaries? Or if he had believed it to be true, would he not have been bound to accept the fashions of his day as the only legitimate expression of the thought and character of his society? No. The principle he tried to apply to all earlier societies, which he had not known at first hand, turned out to be inapplicable to his own. Both architecture and the times were out of joint; wherefore it was plainly the duty of the architect to determine the appropriate basis of a new unity and to set matters aright by building the buildings that would express that unity.

Both architects and the historians of modern architecture have had a vital stake in the validity of Sullivan's proposition. The idea was invented in the eighteenth century, at a time when deep-seated antagonisms were on the verge of shaking European society to its foundations. If the culture or thought of a "people" were really as homogeneous as was averred, then of course there would be no grounds for revolutionary conflict or class struggle. It is but a short and simple step from Sullivan's credo to the notion that by altering a society's architecture one can alter its whole character and outlook. For their not unrelated reasons, both the architect and the cultural historian have felt it necessary to seek out and proclaim, in the face of manifest dissonance and diversity, the underlying unity of our "age." Failing to find evidence thereof in realms of high concern, they have declared it to be the Machine Age; for at least everyone uses machines, even though there may be no common faith or persuasion. And so our architects have striven to express what they hope is the high significance of mechanization in our lives, while the historians of their art have produced volumes of apologetics in an effort at allaying what was initially an overwhelming popular opposition and at winning acceptance for the presumably unifying idea that mechanization has taken command. Partly because of their persuasiveness, the new architecture has carried the day throughout the world; yet now in its hour of triumph, ironically enough, doubts are arising on every hand about the fundamental soundness of the very program that has succeeded so spectacularly. Some of these have been cogently set forth in Lewis Mumford's recent article, "The Case against Modern Architecture." [4]

4. *Architectural Record,* CXXXI (April 1962), 155-62.

In the chapters that follow I propose to consider Wright's work on the basis of other presuppositions. Let me make it plain at the outset that I am well aware of the fact that he was not an utterly isolated phenomenon—that what he was doing in 1905, say, was clearly related to the concerns of a number of other architects, in Chicago, California, Vienna, and elsewhere. However, I would reject the currently popular idea that our understanding of Wright would be greatly enhanced by an exhaustive elucidation of those relationships. There is no doubt some common denominator among Wright, Maher, Purcell, Elmslie, Maybeck, and Greene & Greene; but to isolate and define it would be an essentially reductive process that would probably diminish rather than increase our understanding of those men.

I have undertaken to interpret Wright's architecture mainly in terms of what he himself had to say and in terms of the expressive form of the buildings themselves. My interpretation is neither all-explaining nor definitive. Wright is unique among modern artists in that he has left us both a gigantic *oeuvre* of buildings, projects, and drawings, and also a voluminous body of writing. The buildings are remarkably varied, the writings unsystematic and aphoristic, so that in neither case can one readily abstract anything resembling a unified program or consistent theoretical position. Nevertheless, Wright himself declared that we should expect of an architect "a system of philosophy and ethics." Heretofore he has been dealt with chiefly within the context of the history of modern architecture—influences upon him, his contributions, and so on; whereas one has only to read a few pages of his writings to perceive that ethical considerations were far more important to him than was his relationship to the Modern Movement, whatever that phrase may be taken to designate. Though he was given to making affirmations and denunciations of sweeping grandeur, it was not easy for him to define his position or to state his beliefs clearly. As with other visual artists, his principal statements are in his art; but even these works are endlessly diversified and apparently contradictory.

Those who were close to Wright may feel that my scrutiny of the man and his work is both presumptuous and unnecessary—that the work speaks for itself and does not need to be subjected to interpretative analysis. I am in sympathy with their reservations, for something may well be lost by such examination; but I believe that in the long run a better understanding of Wright will increase our admiration of him. One of my purposes will be to show that he has suffered, perhaps more than any other artist of our time, from being overpraised and underestimated. He has been accorded a vast quantity of adulatory publicity, most of which scarcely touches upon the issues and ideas with which he had to wrestle through his life. His sheer virtuosity in design was such that he may not have seemed to be wrestling at all; yet the ideas were difficult, the solutions sometimes unsatisfactory, and a comprehensive resolution almost impossible of attainment.

Plate I. Self-portrait Photograph by Frank Lloyd Wright, 1895. *Photograph courtesy John Lloyd Wright.*

One of the most conspicuously conservative aspects of his work and thought is that which bears upon the preservation of his image of himself. The nature of that image is revealed most directly in the many portrait photographs Wright made and had made of himself throughout his life. He was intensely aware of his own appearance and, like Rembrandt, liked to strike poses that would reveal what he understood to be his nature.

[*Text reference, page 38*]

Plate II. Portrait of Jean Journet, Lithograph by Gustave Courbet, ca. 1866.

Meyer Shapiro has observed that a close relationship exists between Whitman's conception of the mobile, striding, purposeful, self-reliant writer and the image of the artist that Courbet (who was only eleven days younger than the American poet) set forth in his "Bonjour, M. Courbet." Even more apposite to our concern, perhaps, is the painter's sympathetic portrait of the Fourierist, Jean Journet, "partant pour la conquete de l'harmonie universelle," in that Wright, as the designer of Broadacre City, carried into the twentieth century a tradition of utopian planning in which the name of Fourier looms large.

[*Text reference, page 43*]

Plate III. Seagram Building by Mies van der Rohe, New York, 1958.

Plate IV. Price Tower, Bartlesville, Oklahoma, 1953-55.

The conventional functionalist in present-day architectural practice thinks in Greek, one might say, while Sullivan and Wright thought in Hebrew. What this means in terms of design can best be made clear by a comparison of two buildings, Wright's Price Tower and, say, Mies's Seagram Building. Whereas the latter is a wholly impersonal and objective statement about the possibilities of purity and perfection in design—the purity of an irreducibly simple system of construction and the perfection of a system of proportions—Wright's tower vigorously declares, by means of its rich variations of color, material, shape, saliency, and rhythm, its architect's conviction that life in the modern city—for the doctor and the engineer in their offices no less than for the family in its apartment (the Tower contains both offices and apartments)—should be lively and exciting, touched with novelty and adventure, rising high and proud in the midst of mundane banality.

[*Text reference, pages 57-58*]

Plate V. W. H. Winslow House, River Forest, Illinois, 1893.
Photograph by Thomas A. Heinz.

The Winslow and Ingalls residences, of 1893 and 1909 respectively, mark the limit of formal symmetry and regularity, while the architect's own house and the Robie house, again some sixteen years apart, lie at the opposite end of the scale. In the first pair the architect has established unmistakably the oneness of the house-shape, the dominance of the central axis with reference to which every part is assigned to its place, and the sheltering spread of the single roof beneath which the house is closely contained. In the other two he has created a variable and an unpredictable silhouette, has avoided obvious axiality, has broken the wall structure into

Plate VI. J. Kibben Ingalls House, Oak Park, Illinois, 1909.
Photograph by Thomas A. Heinz.

PLATE VII. FRANK LLOYD WRIGHT'S HOUSE, OAK PARK, ILLINOIS, 1889 WITH LATER ADDITIONS. *Photograph by Thomas A. Heinz.*

planes of various sizes, has assembled those planes so that the pattern of joints seems broken and irregular, and has composed the roof of elements that are differentiated in size, shape, level, and directional axis. In the first pair a close relationship is maintained between the shape of the whole and the shape of the parts, while the parts themselves appear to be relatively few in number and similar in size and form. In the second pair, on the other hand, the shape of the whole bears little resemblance to that of the individual parts, and the number and variety of the parts is conspicuously greater. [*Text reference, pages 78-79*]

PLATE VIII. F. C. ROBIE HOUSE, CHICAGO, ILLINOIS, 1909.
Photograph by Thomas A. Heinz.

PLATE IX. RECEPTION HALL OF THE W. H. WINSLOW HOUSE, RIVER FOREST, ILLINOIS, 1893. *Photograph by the Chicago Architectural Photo Co.*

It is particularly in the design of the reception hall that Wright affirms the sacredness of home and hearth. The room seems hardly to have been designed for family use; it is simply an entrance hall and a connecting space between the living room on the right and the library on the left. Yet it is the most formal, the most carefully articulated room in the house. Behind a delicate wooden arcade, which carries with it something of the sense or flavor of a rood screen before an altar, there lies a brick-walled alcove in the center of which is a broad, square-cut fireplace—large for this period, when most fireplaces were designed for coal grates. It is hard to imagine the area's being used for the ordinary activities of daily life; it looks as if it were intended for the celebration of some solemn family ritual, affirming the sacramental nature of the institution of marriage.

[*Text reference, page 85*]

PLATE X. REAR VIEW OF THE WINSLOW HOUSE. *Photograph by Thomas A. Heinz.*

Only half of the character of the Winslow house is revealed in the street facade, however. Just as important as its formality is the informality of the opposite side of the house, which is broken into a variety of planes at different levels in depth, involves a complicated interplay among rectangular, curving, and polygonal shapes, and is dominated by the off-center stair turret to the same extent as is the other side by the central doorway and chimney. The building confronts the city in one way, the garden in another.

[*Text reference, pages 86-87*]

PLATE XI. THOMAS P. HARDY HOUSE, RACINE, WISCONSIN, 1905.

PLATE XII. FIRST PROJECT FOR MRS. DAVID DEVIN'S HOUSE, 1896.

The houses Wright designed between 1893 and 1909 can be distributed along a line that runs, as it were, from the front of the Winslow house to the back. Closest to the pole of formal regularity lie the first project for Mrs. David Devin's house and the Thomas P. Hardy house. [*Text reference, page 87*]

PLATE XIII. HANDAYU OF NAKA, BY BUNCHO.

Perhaps a word should be said at this point concerning the much-discussed "Japanese influence" in Wright's work, for a number of his drawings are based, as he readily acknowledged, on the style of Japanese prints and screens. Wright repeatedly insisted that he had known nothing of Japanese architecture, other than what he could see in the prints, prior to his first visit to Japan in 1905. I find no reason to quarrel with his account of the matter; for the most striking connections one can point to are to be found, not between Wright's houses and the Japanese house, in all its Mondrianesque simplicity, but rather between his architecture and the style and structure of the Japanese print. (Compare, for instance, the accompanying print by Buncho with Wright's design for the living room of the Heurtley house, plate XV.)

[*Text reference, page 92*]

PLATE XIV. ROBIE HOUSE, DINING ROOM INTERIOR.
Chicago Architectural Photo Co.

One discovers in studying the interiors of these early houses that the polar contrast we have been discussing is manifested again and again in the dissimilar treatment of the dining rooms and the living rooms: the former trend to be as regular as the Winslow façade, the later as irregular as the Glasner house. [Plate XX] As Wright perceived, the occasions of dining and "living" give rise to quite different modes of grouping. At no time do the members of a family exhibit a greater oneness of purpose than in sitting down together for a meal. In his early houses Wright often treated the occasion almost as if it were liturgical in nature; his severely (and uncomfortably) rectilinear furniture, set squarely within a rectilin-

PLATE XV. ARTHUR HEURTLEY HOUSE, OAK PARK, ILLINOIS, 1902. LIVING ROOM INTERIOR. *Grant Manson Collection, Oak Park Public Library.*

ear architectural context, made these dining rooms seem more like stately council chambers than like gathering places for the kind of informal family life we usually associate with Wright's name. In the living room, however, the family is not grouped with reference to a single and definable purpose. Occasionally it may be so, but ordinarily the relation of its members to one another is variable and unpredictable.

[*Text reference, pages 87-89*]

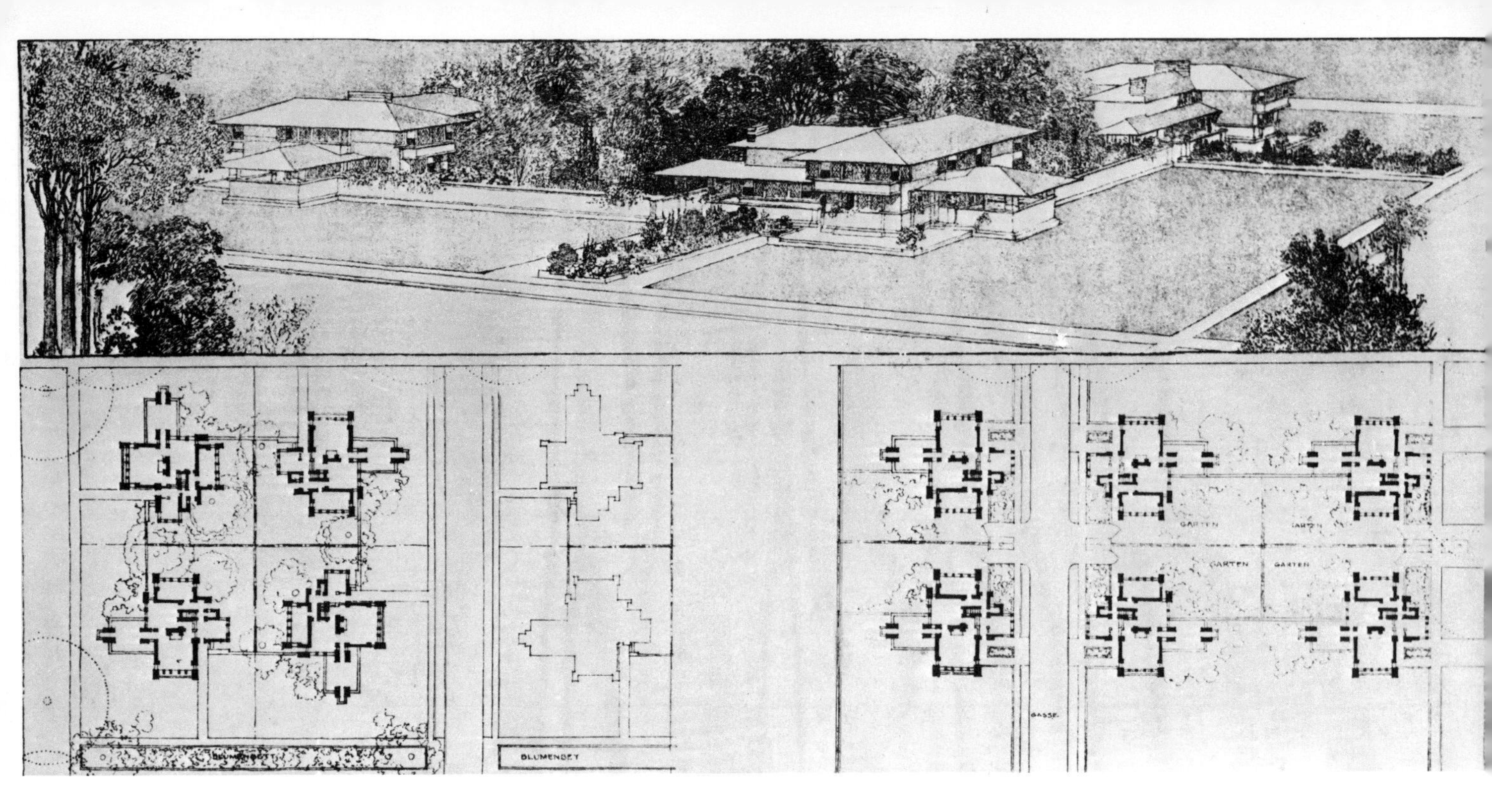

PLATE XVI. QUADRUPLE BLOCK PROJECT, 1902 ET FF.

Around 1900 he began to feel the need for greater uniformity of style and developed what Manson rightly calls the "formula" of the Prairie house, in terms of which most of his designs in the following decade were conceived. From the year of its inception, we discover, he was preoccupied with the idea of grouping together into a larger unit several identical houses of this type. The upshot was the Quadruple Block plan—a scheme with which he was actively concerned for the next ten or fifteen years and with which he tinkered from time to time for the rest of his life. It is not demonstrable that Wright's purpose was a practical one at all. Though the Quadruple Block was exhibited in Chicago as early as 1902, it attracted no backers. The architect never found either four families who wanted identical dwellings or a real estate investor who could believe that a series of such blocks would constitute a salable commodity. For these are not, after all, inexpensive row houses designed for mass production; they are substantial dwellings on half-acre plots. A population density of four families to a block is characteristic only of expensive residential suburbs; but members of the classes that live in such suburbs are precisely the ones who resist most strongly the notion of uniform housing.

[*Text reference, pages 100-101*]

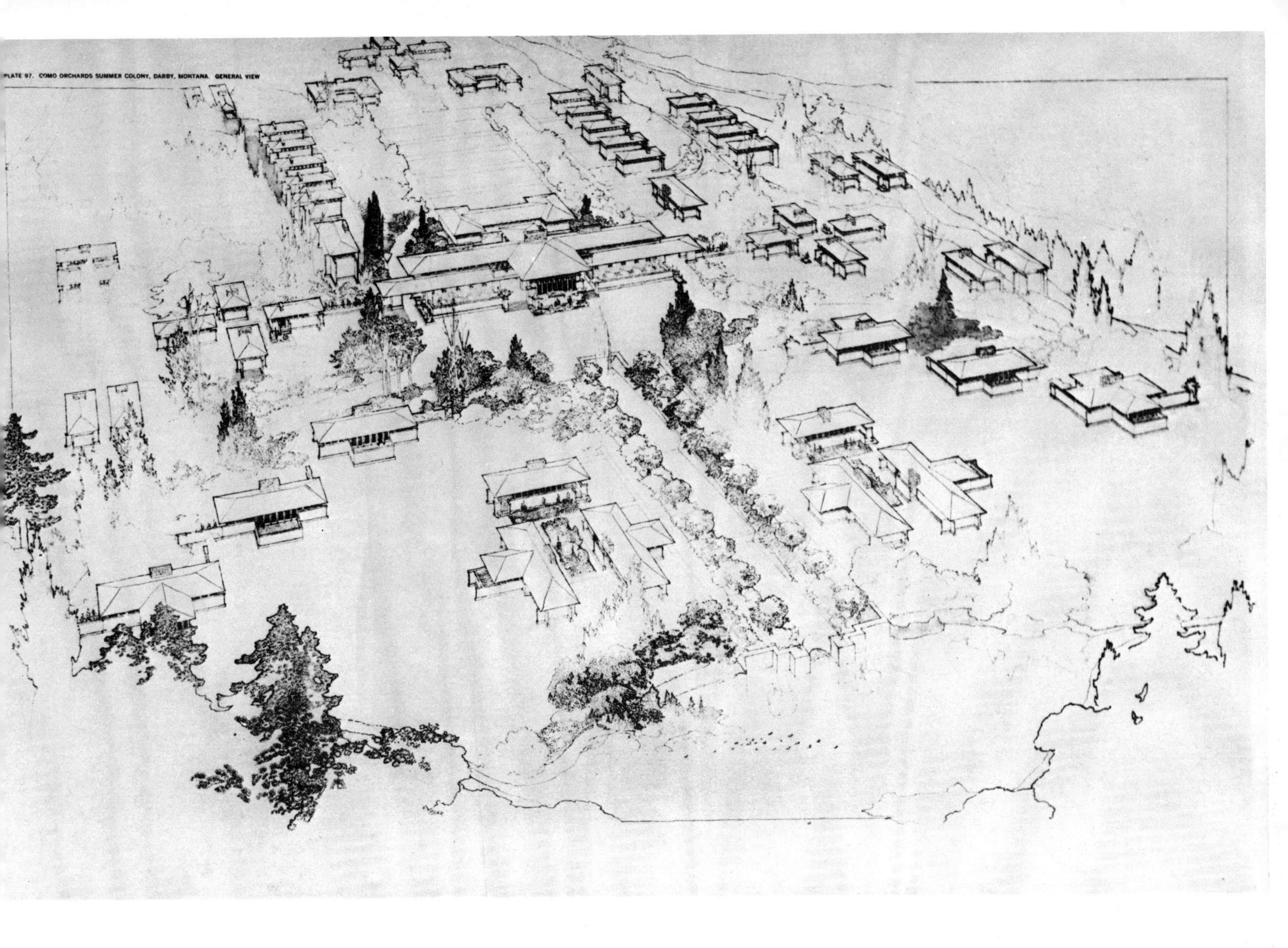

PLATE XVII. COMO ORCHARDS SUMMER COLONY PROJECT, 1909-1910.

Here Wright was asked to design a complete colony of summer residences for a specific site in the Bitter Root Mountains of Montana. The project was initiated by a group of professors from the University of Chicago who intended to develop the colony both as a vacation retreat for themselves and as an economic investment in rental property. As the architect pictured it in 1909, the community would have consisted of fifty-three separate cottages around a great lodge where all the families were to have their meals together. It was to have been a family of families—a purely residential colony in which all the family groups would have assembled at mealtime, just as do the members of a single family at home.

[*Text reference, pages 102-103*]

PLATE XVIII. PRELIMINARY DESIGN, COONLEY HOUSE, RIVERSIDE, ILLINOIS, 1908. *From Frank Lloyd Wright: An American Architecture (1955), courtesy Horizon Press.*

In Mr. Avery Coonley the architect found, or attracted to himself, a new kind of client. Though personally of rather nondescript character and attainment, he was heir to a fortune that provided him with an "independence," the like of which our society has not often seen since the passage of the income tax amendment. In 1906 Mr. Coonley had acquired a tract of several acres in Riverside, and in the following year, as well as can be ascertained, he and his wife (the decision was probably hers) gave Wright virtually *carte blanche* to design as fine a house as he could for them and their one child, Elizabeth, who was then about eight years old. For this family of three the architect produced what Manson aptly describes as the palace of the prairie houses. Within the limits of this relatively small suburban tract (a long oval, the greater part of which has recently been subdivided and studded with small houses), Wright managed to create the semblance of a splendid private estate, complete with stable, cow shed, chicken yard, shop, paddock, gardener's cottage, spacious walled gardens, and an extensive wooded park. With its many projections and recessions, its intricately broken roof line, its colorful wall-tile patterns, and its great profusion of blossoming and trailing plants, the exterior of the house was rich to the point of sumptuousness—and yet surprisingly unpretentious, by reason of its low sprawling form and by virtue of the fact that one cannot see more than a small part of the total structure from any one point of view. Wright describes the Coonley residence as "the most successful of my houses from my standpoint." An illuminating phrase, that—"from my standpoint." Whether or not the house proved satisfactory to the Coonleys we do not know; but then perhaps it was not built for them at all. It was a splendid image, created by its architect to declare his intuitive understanding of what it means for a free man to possess a social space in a spacious and beneficent world; it is the house one feels Wright would have built for himself at that time if he could have afforded to do so—a "populous" house that seems to cry aloud for the presence of a large and noisy family such as his own. (Mr. Coonley was almost exactly the same age as Wright, so it must have been easy for the latter to identify himself with his client.) By contrast, his crowded little house in Oak Park must have seemed insufferably cramped and confining.

[*Text reference, pages 104-107*]

PLATE XIX. H. F. MCCORMICK PROJECT, FOR LAKE FOREST, ILLINOIS, 1907-1908.

Mr. Coonley's affluence was as a drop in the bucket, however, by comparison with that of Wright's other "palace" patron. Harold Fowler McCormick, vice president of the International Harvester Corporation and husband of John D. Rockefeller's daughter, was the principal heir to one of America's gigantic fortunes. He, too, was attracted by Wright's work, and in 1907 he "proposed that [Wright] should present some ideas in sketch form for a new McCormick family seat in Lake Forest, some thirty miles north of Chicago. The site for this project was a large tract of land bordering the bluffs which rise from the beaches of Lake Michigan." This is an extensive a description of the transaction as has even been published; I presume that Manson learned from Wright everything the latter could recall or wanted to recall about this ill-fated undertaking. What was called for was not simply a house for Mr. and Mrs. McCormick but a "family seat"—a building that would serve as a family gathering place and as an adequate symbol of the McCormick's dominant position in the Chicago world. To fulfill these requirements Wright turned to another kind of symbolism and devised a house that would seem rooted in the landscape itself. Toward the lake it was to have raised a façade some three hundred feet wide, rising steeply in three tiers above the precipitous bluffs; while on the opposite side it was to have trailed outward for a hundred and thirty feet or more in three low, rambling extensions that conformed to the rolling shape of the land. But there were difficulties. Mrs. McCormick was opposed to the project from the beginning and refused even to look at his drawings. What she wanted and eventually got was an imposing Italian villa. Although her conduct in this matter, as in others, was not altogether rational, she may have had her reasons; the McCormicks' position in the Chicago world was unquestionably more Medicean than Thoreauistic.

[*Text reference, pages 108-109*]

PLATE XX. W. A. GLASNER HOUSE, GLENCOE, ILLINOIS, 1905.

The first really striking exploitation of the site, however, is achieved in the Glasner cottage at Glencoe, Illinois (1905). The little dwelling was originally to have had a separate tea house across a bridged ravine, but this was never built. Because of the tiny scale and truncated nature of the executed building, little of what Wright had in mind comes through in a photograph. It is rather in the presentational drawing for the house that we find grounds for believing that the architect had now gained an altogether new insight into the possibility of interweaving landscape and architecture. The principle of reciprocity with site stands against the principle by means of which Wright represents urban or communal order. As we have already observed, even the freest of his city houses yet preserves much of the geometrical formality of the straight street and the rectangular block. That the matter is not simply an aesthetic but rather a metaphorical one is demonstrated, it would seem, by the fact that on the rugged site of Como Orchards the architect was prepared to incur the considerable expense of raising many of the fifty-three box-like houses on high basement podia in order to preserve a common roof line between and among those that were to be seen as members of a group: the irregularities of the site were positively an impediment to the proper expression of communality. The Glasner house, by contrast, was a *private* house, set apart from the regularities of the built-up suburb.

[*Text reference, pages 154-55*]

PLATE XXI. TALIESEN I, SPRING GREEN, WISCONSIN, 1911-14. *From Frank Lloyd Wright: An American Architecture (1955), courtesy Horizon Press.*

Taliesen was a rich and subtle embodiment of an idea of which Wright had achieved at best only a partial and inadequate expression heretofore—the idea of a spacious, rambling symbol of the family, rooted not in the arbitrary grid of the city but in Nature itself.

[*Text reference, page 122*]

PLATE XXII. ALINE BARNSDALL-HOLLYHOCK HOUSE, LOS ANGELES, CALIFORNIA, *1920*. West or front elevation after restoration by Lloyd Wright, Frank Lloyd Wright's eldest son. The building is now operated by the City of Los Angeles and is open for tours. *Photograph by Thomas A. Heinz.*

Even before the first of the textile-block residences was undertaken Wright had revealed in his design for the Barnsdall house a taste for impenetrable massiveness and austerity that is quite foreign to his earlier work. We can understand all this in terms of the personal anxieties of the architect, but it is hard to find here an affirmation concerning *res publica* or the image of the family that can be compared to what we see in both earlier and later buildings. He was working in a world to which he felt he did not belong, a world where he had no roots and no place, and where his chief need was not to define the nature of his participation but simply to be sheltered and made secure. This was another house the architect might well have described as being especially satisfactory *from his standpoint;* as with Mr. and Mrs. Coonley, he had found in Miss Barnsdall a client with whom he could readily identify himself, for he was in much the same situation as she. The house was important to him; he devotes ten pages of his *Autobiography* to it.

[*Text reference, pages 125-26*]

PLATE XXIII. EDGAR J. KAUFMANN HOUSE, BEAR RUN, PENNSYLVANIA, 1936.
Photograph by Michael Fedison, courtesy Western Pennsylvania Conservancy.

Wright said that he would like for each of his houses to look as if it could exist nowhere but in the spot where it stands. A relationship of this sort was first adumbrated in such early works as the Glasner house, was fully achieved at Taliesen in 1911, was enunciated as a general principle in the early 1930s, and found its finest expression in the Kaufmann house of 1936. It is still the critical consensus, I believe, that Fallingwater is Wright's most imaginative realization of his conception of the "natural house," built in Nature for the natural man, who himself "shall be like a tree planted by the rivers of water." If ever a house was rooted in the landscape it is this one.

[*Text reference, page 146*]

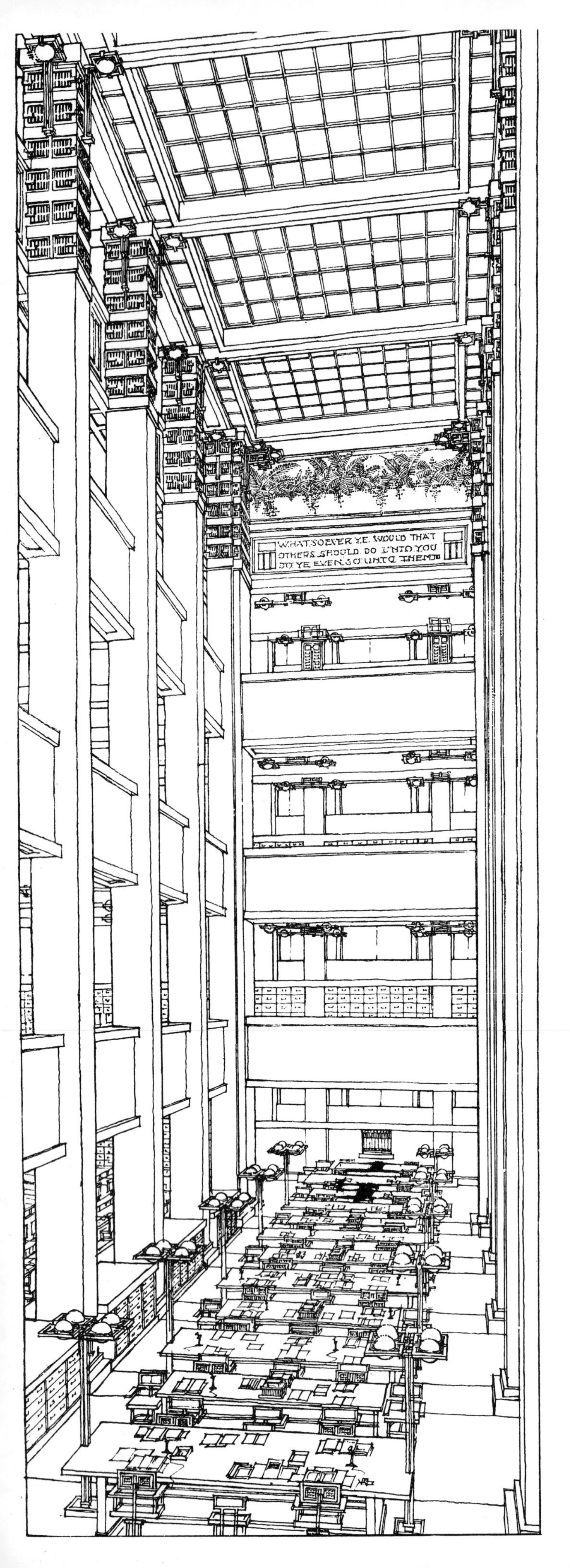

PLATE XXIV. UNITY CHURCH AND COMMUNITY HOUSE, OAK PARK, ILLINOIS, 1906. *From Frank Lloyd Wright: An American Architecture (1955), courtesy Horizon Press.*

PLATE XXV. LARKIN COMPANY ADMINISTRATION BUILDING EXTERIOR, BUFFALO, NEW YORK, 1904. *From Frank Lloyd Wright: An American Architecture (1955), courtesy Horizon Press.*

PLATE XXVI. LARKIN COMPANY ADMINISTRATION BUILDING INTERIOR, BUFFALO, NEW YORK, 1904. *From Frank Lloyd Wright: An American Architecture (1955), courtesy Horizon Press.*

Wright had first become aware of the possibilities of the commercial building when he designed the offices of the Larkin Company in 1904. What with its simplicity, severity, and symmetrical formality, that structure fits easily enough into the sizable class of Wright's public edifices that was discussed in the third chapter. Yet when we compare it with the club houses and apartment buildings from that decade, we see that it possesses an imposing dignity the others generally lack. In part this is due to its size (it is the largest of Wright's early works); but equally important is the framing of the block by the great windowless double pylons—the first about ninety, the second about a hundred feet high—which stood at its four corners. While vertical corner elements of this sort are fairly common in Wright's work prior to 1910, there is only one other structure in which they are used to produce an effect comparable to what we see here—namely, Unity Temple, which was designed in the following year. The kinship between the two buildings is unmistakable.

[*Text reference, page 156*]

FOR THE WORSHIP OF GOD
AND THE SERVICE OF MAN

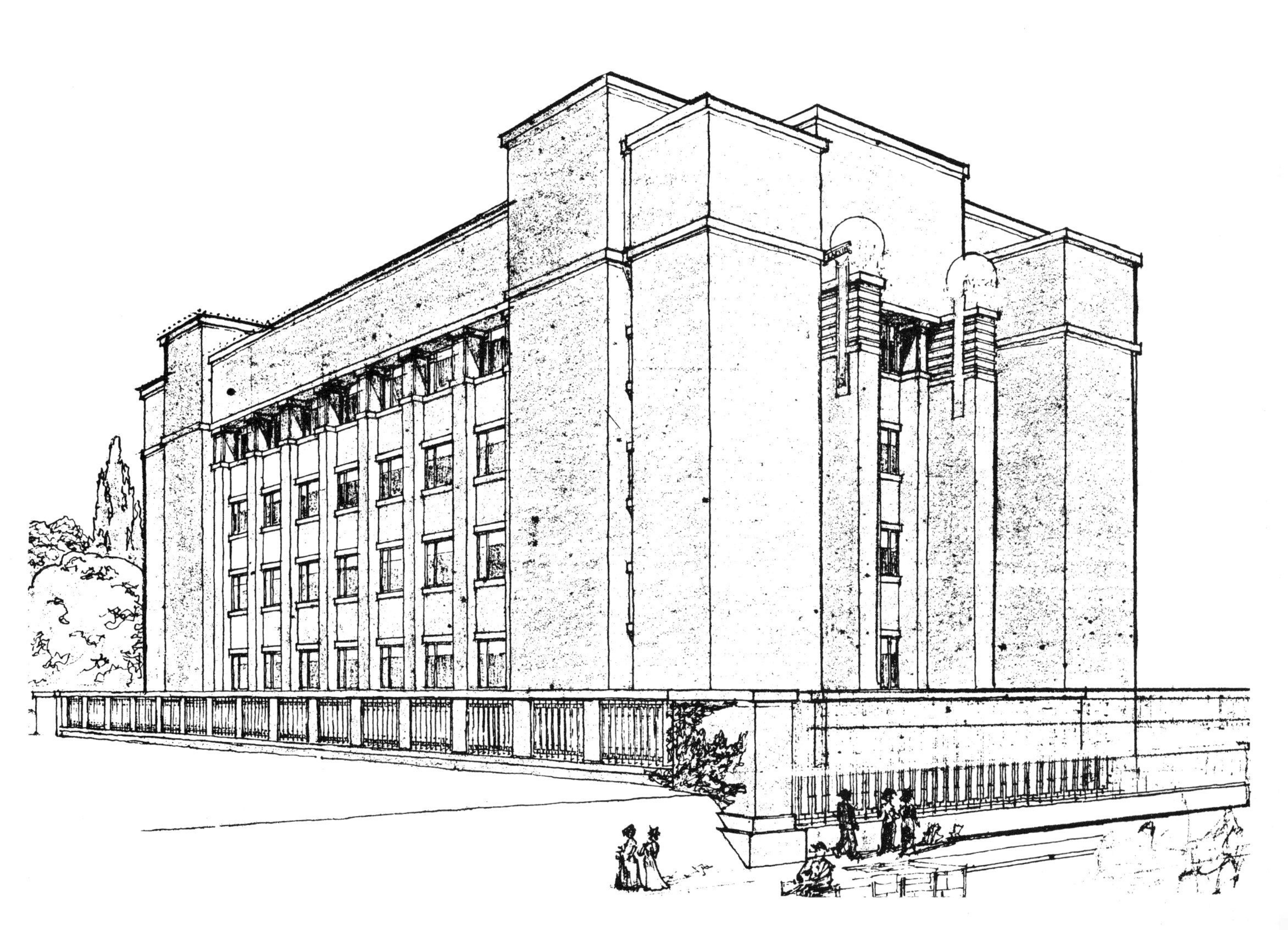

PLATE XXVII. JOHNSON WAX COMPANY, ADMINISTRATIVE OFFICES, RACINE, WISCONSIN, 1936-39.

Although he occasionally described himself as an advocate of "ruralism," his love for the city and for all it represents as a symbol of collective understanding did not diminish and may even have increased in his later years. Of his executed works, the one that expresses most perfectly this aspect of his conviction is the S. C. Johnson & Company administration building in Racine, which was begun in the same year as the Kaufmann house. The two buildings are in many respects diametrically opposite in character. Fallingwater is composed of a great many distinct parts, while the Johnson building is mostly contained within a single molded, flowing wall. The former has projecting members that extend outward in every direction, giving the building a highly irregular silhouette, while the latter is extraordinarily compact and, to use Wright's own word for it, monolithic. Whereas the house is so open as to appear wall-less, the office building is closed within windowless and unbroken masonry. Fallingwater is cantilevered in such a way that it appears to hover without adequate support over the Bear Run ravine, while the Johnson building is planted on heavy foundations and contains a much larger number of columnar supports than is structurally necessary.

[*Text reference, pages 107-109*]

PLATE XXVIII. MADONNA AND CHILD WITH SAINTS AND ANGELS, BY PIERO DELLA FRANCESCA. *Brera Gallery, Milan.*

In a context of windowless "total architecture" Piero celebrates the virtues of membership, of unqualified involvement within a closed and eternally stable society, of submission to the regulatory discipline of the Sovereign. The six saints who form the Virgin's court can be identified by name, but they could be replaced by any other six one might care to select. St. Francis appears here wholly as a member, his position being interchangeable with that of any other citizen of the celestial kingdom. Piero places his figures in a palace, therefore at the heart of the city and at the seat of government.

[*Text reference, page 178*]

PLATE XXIX. JOHNSON WAX COMPANY, EXTERIOR DETAIL.

We must go one step further and consider the two images of paradise which have persisted side by side in Christian thought: heaven as a garden and heaven as a strong city—the New Eden and the New Jerusalem. This is the framework within which Wright made his prophetic avowals. The city declares ultimate blessedness to be one of perfect mutuality—of membership and security within an enclosed setting of steadfast order. At this pole stand the voluntary group, working together in a common cause in the midst of the city, which is itself identified with the binding functions of civilization and a common culture. Its building is closed and fortress-like, showing forth the nature of the city as "ein feste Burg."

[*Text reference, pages 178-79*]

PLATE XXX. ST. FRANCIS IN ECSTACY, BY GIOVANNI BELLINI. *Copyright, Frick Collection, New York.*

Bellini celebrates the utterly unique and intensely personal religious experience—a moment of agonizing poignancy that comes to the saint when he is alone in the midst of nature. A Wordsworth or a Thoreau could have added nothing whatever to Bellini's presentation of that experience, in which the smallest leaf and pebble are shown to be "apparelled in celestial light." Bellini states explicitly, as other painters of the subject had not done, that St. Francis received his transfiguring vision outside and away from the city.

[*Text reference, page 178*]

PLATE XXXI. KAUFMANN HOUSE, EXTERIOR DETAIL.

We must go one step further and consider the two images of paradise which have persisted side by side in Christian thought: heaven as a garden and heaven as a strong city—the New Eden and the New Jerusalem. This is the framework within which Wright made his prophetic avowals. The garden represents ultimate blessedness as the enjoyment of perfect freedom in a setting of unlimited horizontal expanse and of the most varied and sensuous delights. At this pole stands the intimate private family, a handful of persons whose relationship to one another is marked by spontaneous delight: it is natural, growing, changing, dynamic, free—as open and as variable as the landscape itself. The nature in the midst of which the family dwells is no mere composite of biological phenomena; it is Isaiah's nature, in which the very hills may break forth into singing and the trees of the field clap their hands. The family's house lies far from the city and deep in the woodlands that are held to be, in essence, a paradisiacal garden.

[*Text reference, pages 178-79*]

ONE

THE CAUSE CONSERVATIVE

TO FIND OUT WHAT I TAKE TO BE THE ESSENTIAL idea that has been overlooked in the architectural apologetics of the Modern Movement, let us go back to the first words of Wright's first important essay on architecture, which was published in the spring of 1908: "Radical though it be, the work here illustrated is dedicated to a cause conservative in the best sense of the word." [1] The idea of the "cause conservative" was uppermost in Wright's mind, but it is precisely this idea that has been ignored in the theoretical writings that have accompanied the promotion of contemporary style.

The Metaphor of the State

In his interesting essay on architecture in the *Encyclopedia of World Art,* Bruno Zevi takes up the question of what, if anything, is unique or distinctive about the art of architecture, effectively dismisses various aesthetic and historicist theories that have been proposed, and concludes, to the surprise of no one who is familiar with his writings, that its uniqueness lies in its being able to surround the observer with shaped space. Throughout his analysis of the theory and history of the art, Zevi finds it unnecessary to make use of the word "institution." One can agree with him that there is no need for developing a special architectural aesthetic, his spatial one included; but it is hard to escape the fact that the buildings that have traditionally been regarded as works of architectural art have invariably been bound up with an organized social group, an established institution.

According to Nikolaus Pevsner, "A bicycle shed is a building, Lincoln Cathedral is a piece of architecture. . . . The term architecture applies only to buildings designed with a view to aesthetic appeal." Zevi disputes this, contending, rightly enough, that a bicycle shed may be designed so as to be aesthetically appealing. But would this make it a work of architectural art? I think not, because it would still be unrelated to any kind of institutional meaning. Palace, house, tomb, capitol, court, temple, church—these, mainly, are the buildings which stand for the institutionalized patterns of human relatedness that make pos-

1. Frank Lloyd Wright, "In the Cause of Architecture," *Architectural Record,* XXIII: 3 (March 1908), 155.

sible the endurance of the city, or of society, or of the state; and these have provided almost all the occasions for meaningful architectural art for the past five thousand years. They bear upon realms of experience that have given rise to great quantities of painting and poetry; but one would be hard put to find either a painter or a poet who could make much out of the occasion or the experience of bicycle-parking. Nor can the architect endow it with significance.

If, of course, one accepts at face value the modern hypostatization of the idea of style and, in keeping with historicist doctrine, interprets every style as constituting a distillation of that transcendent and quasi-Platonic reality known as the "Zeitgeist" or "the times" or "the culture," then one may dispute this assertion and maintain that every building designed in a given style, be it bicycle shed or cathedral, is a visible concretion of the homogeneous spiritual entity that Sullivan called "the thought of a people." For my part, I reject such historicism out of hand, seeing no reason to believe that such an entity exists or has ever existed. Men do not understand or agree with one another that well. While many a modern architect has dreamed of erecting a purely modern city in which every building, from the smallest to the largest, would exemplify the same universally modern style, the dream is fatuously empty, since it ignores entirely the way cities and people exist in historical time. One may imagine a timeless Heavenly Jerusalem, as Le Corbusier was given to doing in the 1920s; but like Plato in Syracuse, Le Corbusier discovered (without ever understanding why it should have been the case) that although his vision may have seemed inspiring to a few architectural historians and other cloistered academics, it was wholly unacceptable to those who were actually responsible for making decisions within the fractious context of factious public life. Some may think that the existence of Brasilia proves me wrong; but it seems to me that the very fact that that city now houses a peculiarly corrupt and oppressive government demonstrates the fatuousness of the architects' dream, or at least their failure to grasp the fact that an oceanic chasm separated their thinking from that of the political leaders of Brazil.

We need to take account of the fact that architecture is uniquely the art of urban society, rather than of tribal or earlier associations. The latter may have traditional and attractive ways of building, but the inventive architectural artist appears on the scene after the emergence of the great river-valley civilizations around 3000 B.C. Architecture is to be found only in those societies, it would seem, in which the individual possesses enough freedom and self-consciousness to pursue private goals and to contemplate his relationship to the state from a personal and potentially disaffected point of view.[2] Ever since its grandiose beginnings in Egypt, when, during the Third Dynasty, the Old Kingdom was losing its monolithic cohesiveness, architecture has been employed in defense of social stability against threats of divisiveness, schism, rebellion, usurpation, heresy, and so on. One thinks immediately of the colossal halls that were erected following the suppression of Akhnaten's upsetting reforms (which, since they were the work of a king, had their own architectural expression, though a relatively ephemeral one); of the fact that the Parthenon was finished just one year before the political situation in Greece dissolved into disastrous civil war in which Athens was ruined; of the mighty works of Roman architecture that arose during the century-long period of disruption that extends from the time of Caracalla to that of Constantine; of Justinian's great church that was begun only six weeks after the destruction of an earlier building in the course of city-wide rioting that threatened to oust the emperor from his throne; of the magnificent architectural defense of the institution of monasticism that was made in the twelfth century when that institution was already declining and in constant need of reform; of the connection between the outbreak of the Reformation and the rebuilding of St. Peter's Basilica on a grander scale than any that man had previously envisioned; and of other examples too numerous to mention.

To put it bluntly, architecture has always been the art of the Establishment. It has been bought and paid for exclusively by successful, prosperous, property-owning institutions with a stake in the preservation of the status quo, and it has generally exhibited its greatest power and originality at times when those institutions have been threatened and in need of support. Needless to say, the other arts have

2. For some interesting suggestions concerning the relation of architecture to the inherent self-destructiveness of cities, *vide* Herbert J. Muller, *The Uses of the Past* (New York: Oxford University Press, 1953), Chap. 1.

also been patronized by members of those institutions. The uniqueness of architecture lies in the fact that it is *about* the institutional establishment, as the other arts generally are not, though on occasion they may be.

It has often been observed that architecture is the most impersonal or least expressive of the arts, for which reason Hegel placed it at the lowest or "symbolic" level in his hierarchy of art forms. The observation is rankling to some enthusiasts, who see no reason why there should not arise an Abstract Expressionist architecture to match the painting of recent years. Yet it goes without saying that institutions do not themselves experience, nor do they chiefly exist in order to cause their members to experience, ecstasy or nostalgia, grief or laughter, compassion or despair. An institution is not a person; it is an established framework, a pattern of relatedness among men, a mode of grouping within which the individual experiences membership and finds some basis for making decisions, passing judgments, determining goals. Like a building, the institution claims for itself a size and a power to endure which greatly exceed those of the ephemeral human being. By virtue of its size, its stability, and its permanence, it is able to shelter and to protect its members, not simply from the elements but from that destructive individualization, that "scattering abroad upon the face of all the earth," with which every urban society is in some measure threatened. A building may be said to be a work of architectural art, then, insofar as it serves as a visual metaphor, declaring in its own form something (though never everything) about the size, permanence, strength, protectiveness, and organizational structure of the institution it stands for (but does not necessarily house).

There is good reason to believe that Wright understood from the beginning of his career, as Louis Sullivan never understood, the relation of architectural metaphor to the state and to the lesser institutions of which its fabric is made up. As early as 1900 he wrote that "civilization must take the natural man to fit him for his place in this great piece of architecture we call the social state." [3] Later he declared that

3. Frank Lloyd Wright, "Japanese Prints," reprinted in Frederick A. Gutheim, *Frank Lloyd Wright on Architecture* (New York: Duell, Sloane, and Pearce, 1941), p. 23.

"since all form is a matter of structure, it is a matter of government as well as a matter of architecture; a matter of the framework of a society." [4] It was this relationship between institutional pattern and architectural form, as Wright saw it, which had always made architecture an expression of "the spirit of law and order."

Yet I do not mean to imply that his essential concern was with the government of the United States. Like Sullivan, Wright was a reformer. He did not esteem the present order of things, but rather looked forward always to the realization of an ideal society that he believed to be within our reach. Not the government but the ethical problem of right governance was at the heart of his concern.

Wright thus recovered an understanding of the nature of architecture which had been all but lost during the nineteenth century, when the art of building had come to be put to a novel and quite different use: namely, that of conjuring up, in the single observer, emotionally charged associations with one or another of the great "ages" in the historical world-drama. It seems generally to have been supposed that each of those ages (which could be likened to the movements of a titanic symphony) had possessed a unique spirit or rhythm or tonality of its own; that the architect's function had been to "express" that spirit in visible forms; and, moreover, that a great building could somehow arouse or inculcate a corresponding spiritual attitude in a modern person—whence the enthusiasm for building Gothic churches in the days of Pugin and Ruskin. In all this the structure-giving role of the institution was made secondary to, or wholly eliminated in favor of, the emotional experience of the individual.

It is usually taken for granted today that the distinctively modern architecture of the present century had its origins in a drastic reaction against this nineteenth-century aberration. I would argue, on the contrary, that our mechanistic contemporary style is based on the same Victorian presuppositions about architecture as undergirded the Gothic revival more than a century ago: it results, that is, from a self-conscious attempt by the architect to invent a style that will express what he presumes to be the unifying spirit of his age and that will at the same time (paradoxically enough) propagate and inculcate that same spirit in a

4. *Autobiography*, p. 380.

recalcitrant populace which grievously lacks it and reveals, instead, a distressing inclination toward the emotional irrationalities of nationalism and of war. His concern for institutional metaphor, however, is no greater than was his eclectic predecessor's. Wright, on the other hand, was a builder of institutional symbols.

The Gentleman Architect

BUT WHY a cause *conservative*? In one of its meanings the word conservative designates a manner or attitude that stands opposed to extravagance, risk-taking, immoderation, and the like. One's first inclination is to dismiss this sense of the word as being wholly inapplicable to Wright, what with his flamboyant bravura, his conspicuously eccentric dress, and his monetary profligacy. However, the publicity that his eccentricities and iconoclastic pronouncements invited has quite overshadowed his innate conservatism.

The trait revealed itself early. In the spring of 1887, toward the end of his second year at the University of Wisconsin, Wright came to Chicago with the intention of becoming an architect. The story of his first years there is well known, but perhaps its implications have not been rightly gauged. In order to understand the nature of the role Wright wanted to play, it is instructive to compare his reaction to the city with that of Theodore Dreiser, who reached Chicago at about the same time. Son of a bigotedly Catholic German immigrant, Dreiser had always felt himself, while growing up in a small-town, middle-western, Protestant environment, to be an "outsider," and it was as such that he viewed Chicago. He was entranced with the busy, colorful, brightly lighted big city, but he was at the same time very much aware of its slums and of the misery of the poor who were, in a sense, outsiders like himself.

Wright, on the other hand, had no eye at all for the slums. Instead, he was offended by the garish signs, the glaring arc-lamps, the "brutal hurrying crowd intent on seeing nothing," the ubiquitous saloons, the noise, the foreign names—by the rank vulgarity and tastelessness of the burgeoning city. His judgment was essentially that of an "insider," little though he may have felt himself to be one at that point; it was the judgment of one who knew himself rightfully to belong, despite his poverty, to what he was later to describe as an "innate aristocracy" of cultivated and responsible persons.

Let us see what he liked. On the fourth day after his arrival he found a job, at eight dollars a week, in the office of J. L. Silsbee.

> He was building my uncle's "All Souls" church, but he needn't know who I was. After noon I went there. Liked the atmosphere of the office best. Liked Silsbee's sketches on the wall. Liked instantly the fine-looking, cultured fellow with a pompadour and beard, who came forward with a quiet smile—Cecil Corwin. . . . He looked the artist-musician. Through the outer office railing he had come humming from the "Messiah." [5]

The addition of Wright brought to five the number of minister's sons in the office—a detail that reveals a great deal about the class of conservative and institutionally oriented persons to whom the architect's profession was, and perhaps still is, attractive. Among the five was Silsbee himself, whom Corwin described to Wright as

> "a kind of genius; but something is the matter with him. He doesn't seem to take any of it or to take himself half seriously. The picture interests him. The rest bores him. You'll see. He's an architectural genius spoiled by way of the aristocrat. A fine education and family in Syracuse, but too contemptuous of everything." And I did see. . . . But I adored Silsbee just the same. He had style.[6]

Soon Wright was working for another haughty, contemptuous employer, Louis Sullivan, and was fast developing an aristocratic "style" of his own which remained one of his most distinctive characteristics throughout his life.

Within a week after his arrival he had associated himself with the activities of a cultivated upper-middle-class circle that was centered about his uncle's fashionable Unitarian church. Within less than three years he had married the daughter of a successful businessman (a young lady "whose ancestors had landed on Plymouth Rock") and had established his residence in the respectable suburb of Oak Park. And within four years we find him designing works such as the Charnley house (1891).

5. *Ibid.*, pp. 67-68.
6. *Ibid.*, p. 71.

If we consider this building from the standpoint of the historian of modern style, we may think it radically progressive, a forerunner of the simplified, planimetric structures of the International Style. The weakness of this kind of analysis lies in the fact that it distracts our attention from the individual building and from the immediate situation in which it was conceived, and directs it instead toward the relationship of isolated features of one building to isolated features of other buildings that were later created by other men in other circumstances in other parts of the world. These features are taken out of their context and arranged in chronological order to exemplify what is hypostatized as "the evolution of modern style." What results is a tendency to give a higher reality and importance to an elusive (and perhaps illusory) process than to the single, concrete work of art. Thus one inevitably loses sight of the motivations of the particular architect on a given and specific occasion.

But if we put aside the notion that modern architecture is intrinsically progressive and therefore liberal, and consider only the affective and organizational characteristics of the Charnley house *per se,* we recognize at once that it is austerely conservative in design—in that sense of the word that connotes temperance, propriety, restraint, and abste-

miousness. One knows it to be the work of a man of fastidious taste. His purposes can be fully understood not by looking forward to the Villa Savoye but by looking backward to the immediately preceding decade and comparing the house to one that typifies the rankly ostentatious taste of the 1870s and '80s. If M. E. Bell's Mary Wilke house (1889) may be regarded as a last manifestation of the old expansiveness, then the Charnley house as clearly exemplifies the new conservatism that was already everywhere in evidence when Wright reached Chicago—as one may see by glancing through any volume of the *Inland Architect* of around 1890.

Wright's earliest works were apparently built almost in the shadow of Victorian mansions even fussier than Bell's—houses like "the old Scovill place, occupying a whole square of the town [of Oak Park], standing there shamelessly tall, to say the last word for the depravity characterizing the residence architecture of that period." [7] Wright's use of the words "shameless" and "depravity" seems a little prim. His reaction to the mores of the preceding generation is similar in many ways to that of his older contemporary and fellow Wisconsonian, Thorstein Veblen, who was much more deeply offended by the competitive extravagance of the rich than by the poverty of an exploited working class. To this new generation, for which Theodore Roosevelt would soon emerge as spokesman, the concept of *conservation* was to become enormously important, in reaction against the profligacy of the era of Jay Gould and the Vanderbilts.

One may think it straining an etymological relationship to link conservation with conservatism, but Wright understood the connection perfectly well.

> Gables, dormers, minarets, bays, porches, oodles of jiggered woodwork ruthlessly painted, poking in or peeking out of piles of fancified stonework and playing idiotic tricks with each other, just to captivate the eye? Oh, no; just to inflate some well-to-do owner's sense of himself—the owneress as she saw "himself." . . . The pernicious social fabric so excruciated by adornment was a moral, social, aesthetic excrement that was only the rubbish heap of *a nationwide waste of all natural resources.* As for sensitive aesthetics, the whole town from any sane point of view was obscene for everybody in it and all truths of being except one: vulgarity. . . . Stupid? No. Just wicked *extravagance* passing for luxury—advertising to posterity that its owners were not on speaking terms with either scholars or gentlemen.[8]

Wright's notion of a gentleman would have been epitomized in Theodore Roosevelt, whose concern for honor, integrity, and the public welfare stemmed from his gentlemanly *noblesse,* which was conservative to the core.

One thing that made Wright's architecture and his way of being an architect so different from Sullivan's is that he had a different kind of stake in, or attitude toward, the middle-class establishment. Both of Sullivan's parents were recent immigrants—his mother from Switzerland, his father from Ireland at a time when the Irish were decidedly unpopular in New England, where the architect was born. Wright, on

7. *Ibid.*, p. 79.
8. Frank Lloyd Wright, *Genius and Mobocracy* (New York: Duell, Sloane, and Pearce, 1949), pp. 32-33.

the other hand, knew himself to be related, on his father's side, to such pillars of respectability as the Lowells of Boston and, on his mother's, to a well-rooted clan of Wisconsin farmers and preachers. For Sullivan architecture seemed to afford a means whereby the "feudalism" of the existing social order could be transformed, by little more than environmental conditioning, into an ideal "democracy." Wright imbibed great draughts of this Whitmanesque philosophy from Sullivan, yet the nature of his commitment was essentially different. Sullivan consistently sought, and was at his best in dealing with, work that had little or nothing to do with the traditional and institutionalized values of his society. We associate his name with skycrapers, department stores, hotels, banks, and theaters (speculative commercial ventures, all), but not with the domestic, civic, and religious institutions that for ages on end have had to do with the maintenance of civil decorum. From first to last Wright was drawn to just those occasions and was concerned with a social ideal of harmonious consistency and stability.

But though he wanted to be esteemed a cultivated and distinguished artist-architect, and had aspirations that were eventually realized in his playing the role of country squire in the grand manner, at the beginning of his career he lacked the "social credentials" that might have made him attractive to the suburban establishment of Evanston and the North Shore. He had come, after all, from a poor and provincial family; lacking even a high school diploma, he had been able to acquire only a few months of mainly technical education at the college level. As Leonard K. Eaton has ascertained, his early clients were mainly "self-made" businessmen, mostly engaged in technical lines of work.[8] They were in somewhat the same social position as he was, wherefore he undertook to express their shared kind of conservatism in terms that did not involve learned allusions to an ancestral past. The decorous propriety that was made manifest in his domestic interiors was *sui generis*: in no way did it depend upon, or even admit the possibility of, the incorporation of family tradition by way of inherited "antiques." Not only was old furniture excluded but also old

8a. Cf. Leonard K. Eaton, *Two Chicago Architects and their Clients: Frank Lloyd Wright and Howard Van Doren Shaw* (Cambridge, Mass.: M.I.T. Press, 1969).

works of art. If one of his clients had been so fortunate as to own a Rembrandt or a Gainsborough, he would have discovered that there was hardly any place in the house where it could even have been hung, and no place where it would have fitted in in such a way as to enhance, and to be enhanced by, the architectural context.

Wright knew perfectly well for whom he was working and wanted to work. He understood both the strengths and the limitations of his clientele.

> Even cultured men and women care so little for the spiritual integrity of their environment. . . . A structure has no more meaning to them aesthetically than has a stable to a horse. And this came to me in the early years as a definite discouragement. There were exceptions, and I found them chiefly among American men of business with unspoiled instincts and untainted ideals. A man of this type usually has the faculty of judging for himself. . . . He errs on the side of character at least; . . . he will be regarded as the true conservator.[9]

Kuno Francke had misunderstood. Wright's orientation was not mainly toward the future, toward the progressive unfolding of twentieth-century modernity; rather it was toward lending a new kind of respectability, a newly defined kind of status, to a class of "rugged individualists" whom he regarded as being the very backbone of American business. He knew as clearly as did the architects of Seti I and Rameses II that his patrons were *conservators*.

An Art of the Home

AN EQUALLY familiar meaning of the word conservative makes it more or less synonymous with preservative. The conservative, in this sense, is one who wishes to preserve from change the existing institutions of social order; he is the opposite of the revolutionist. Again, one's first impulse is to deny that the word is applicable to Wright, for he was not in the least given to venerating the status quo, but rather denounced it as iniquitous at every opportunity. But though he inclined somewhat toward the ideals of anarchism, he was not a revolutionist; he was an architect. That is to say, he was a *builder*; his outlook was *constructive*; he was not an overturner. As he said of his own work, "At no

9. "In the Cause of Architecture," 1908, p. 158.

point does it involve denial of the elemental law and order inherent in all great architecture; rather, it is a declaration of love for the spirit of that law and order, and a reverential recognition of the elements that made its ancient letter in its time vital and beautiful." [10] Unlike Sullivan, he was profoundly concerned with the organizational function, and so with the ethical implications, of the institutions for which he designed buildings—though not in every case, perhaps, nor always to the same degree.

In fact, there was only one institution with which he was deeply and continuously concerned throughout his life, and that was the family. In his last book (1958) he wrote, "The true center (the only centralization allowable) in Usonion democracy is the individual in his true Usonian family home. In that we have the nuclear building we will learn how to build." [11] Even then the problem was alive and unresolved; we *will* learn to cope with it.

Despite the fact that he was the protégé of an architect who generally refused to design residences, Wright was mainly a builder of private homes even before his break with Adler & Sullivan. Residential commissions which the firm could not refuse were often turned over to him; others he accepted privately in violation of his contract—a violation which led to his abrupt separation from the firm in 1893. One may argue, of course, that this indicates nothing more than that the important commercial and industrial commissions of the day were going to the established leaders of the "Chicago School," and that Wright and other members of the younger generation had to content themselves with the crumbs brushed from their table. No doubt Wright would have been pleased and flattered if the first client to enter his office in 1893 had requested a multi-million-dollar skyscraper rather than a modest suburban home. It seems reasonably clear, however, that he chose to conduct his practice in such a way as not to attract a commercial clientele. Indeed, he states explicitly that that was a world with which he could have no affinity.

10. *Ibid.*, p. 155.
11. Frank Lloyd Wright, *The Living City* (New York: Horizon Press, 1958), p. 207.

The relation of the architect to the economic and industrial movement of his time, in any fine art sense, is still an affair so sadly out of joint that no one may easily reconcile it. All agree that something has gone wrong and except the architect be a plain factory magnate, who has reduced his art to a philosophy of old clothes and sells misfits or made-over-ready-to-wear garments . . . he cannot succeed on the present basis established by common practice.[12]

Throughout his life Wright tended increasingly to attribute an opprobrious meaning to the word "commercial." To think that he would have liked to be a Louis Sullivan if he had been given a choice is to miss the point and purpose of his architecture.

In his life-long preference for domestic building there is revealed a great deal about the concern, or complex of concerns, that underlies his art. Something of the peculiar importance we feel his work to possess is surely due to the urgency of that concern, not only for him but for modern Americans generally; for we are much aware of the difficulties that presently plague the life of the family, of the problematical nature of conjugal and parental relationships, and of the responsibilities and failures of the family in connection with various ills that infect our society.

In order to understand the significance of Wright's inventions one must take some account of the fact that throughout the nineteenth century the institution of the family was sporadically subjected to attack by reformers such as Robert Owen, who denounced marriage as a chief impediment to the enjoyment of liberty; that the whole theory and nature of the family were matters of far-ranging sociological, anthropological, and psychological investigation; and that it was widely believed that a progressive relaxation or dropping of family bonds was both desirable and inevitable, the logical consequence of the growth of personal freedom and the decline of institutionalism in our society.

A telling indication of this crisis of the family is to be found in the development of modern art. From about 1860 onward there appear many indications of a growing uneasiness about the family and its mode of relatedness. One sees them in the work of artists as various as Manet, Degas, Van Gogh, and Munch, and of writers such as Ibsen, Strindberg, and Samuel Butler. In the course of Wright's lifetime

12. "In the Cause of Architecture," 1908, p. 159.

familial themes disappeared almost entirely from Western painting. Gentle and agreeable family scenes were still appealing to Monet and Renoir (though rarely do they involve a complete family group) ; but after 1895 domestic themes all but vanish. In the painting of the present century, both European and American, the ethical ideal that centers upon the family hearth and board and upon the relationship of father and son and of mother and child has given way to an individualistic and experiential concern to which institutionalization of any and every sort is irrelevant.

Yet the disappearance of familial themes from modern art should not be taken to mean that the family no longer matters. The artist does not "mirror his times" or simply make known to us a factual situation. Despite his indifference toward domesticity, the family is still the most powerful and influential institution in our society, being principally responsible for civilizing the young; so that when even a tiny proportion of the total number of families fails in this responsibility, the supplemental and correctional facilities of the state prove hopelessly inadequate. Especially in the United States has there been broad popular resistance to the ethical reorientation the painter has espoused. The traditional American symbol of the independent family, the detached private house set within its private yard, has remained attractive to millions of people, even when reduced to the diminutive scale of the developer's "ranch house" and despite the attacks that have been directed against its inefficiency and its architectural sterility by planners and critics.

In our American world, moreover, the emotionally charged conception that is embodied in the untranslatable word "home" has taken on an increasing importance among ethical and organizational principles, coloring our attitudes toward aspects of our experience other than those that pertain strictly to the life of the family. Consider, for instance, that peculiarly American invention, the "funeral home"—an establishment that typically occupies a spacious, old-fashioned house of a kind that better suits a popular conception of an ideal family home than do the houses we actually construct for ourselves. It makes evident the shift that has taken place in the locus of certain fundamental values, from the public or communal institution of the church to the more personal institution of the family.

But then the church itself has changed. The phrase "church home" is often heard today in Protestant parlance, especially among the members of suburban churches. What it connotes is radically different in meaning from the *domus domini* of the Middle Ages. Whereas the *domus* is a symbol of institutional power, containing the throne of an ecclesiastical lord to whose prestige and authority the building attests, the "church home" is conceived to be an intimate fellowship of congenial members who address one another and their pastor by their first names—a *tutoiement* that would have been unthinkable in an earlier age when the parson was set apart from the laity by education, dress, and manner.[13]

The new American usage betokens a mode of relatedness which constitutes the very core of the ethical ideal that the suburban citizen expects the church to uphold. Like all metaphors, "church home" points in two directions: it implies not only that there is something home-like about the church but also that there is something church-like about the home. For it is the home that is conceived to exercise in our society the kind of organizational primacy that in times past has been claimed by other institutions—tribe, clan, village, polis, monastery, church, and so on. The small private family began to take on this wider significance early in the fifteenth century. Concurrently, painters turned toward looser and less architectonic compositions and made rapid progress in the development of landscape and portraiture. From the beginning these changes were bound up with a new evaluation of the nature and importance of the single person and of his ability to comprehend, to make decisions within, and to exert control over the world as he directly experiences it.

13. A similar quasi-familial intimacy apparently existed among the members of the Apostolic Church, who assembled at times in private houses and who attached great importance to experiences of eating and singing together. Later, and especially after the accession of Constantine, the form of the church was assimilated to that of the imperial state. Only then did the need for church architecture arise; for only those institutions that are on the side of the state—only *legal* institutions—can make use of architectural symbolism, an essential purpose of which is to demonstrate the relation of the commissioning institution to the larger fabric of the city, which in turn provides us with our only viable image of the state.

In the sixteenth and seventeenth centuries, when painters were devoting their best efforts to the development of the new *genres* we have just mentioned, architects were busily defending the conservative institutions of Roman church and absolute monarchy, refurbishing and restating the symmetrical, legalistic, and hierarchical patterns they had received from the Middle Ages.[14] With the advent of the radically modern art of the late nineteenth and early twentieth centuries, however, which heralded the imminent disappearance of landscape, portraiture, and even still life from the canvases of preeminent artists within Wright's own lifetime, it fell to the architect to defend just those values which the painter had espoused some three hundred years earlier. The conservative problem with which Wright found it necessary to wrestle was that of redefining and reaffirming the significance of familism at a time when it seemed, as Bertrand Russell later asserted, "inevitable, for good or evil, that the family as a unit should more and more fade away, leaving no group to interpose its authority between the individual and the State." [15]

14. The most instructive comparison one can make, so far as I know, is between the works of Palladio and those of Tintoretto. The two men were born in the same year, 1518, and spent their lives working in the same district and sometimes, as in the case of San Giorgio Maggiore, for the same patrons. When we compare Palladio's Villa Rotunda or one of his church façades with Tintoretto's "Last Supper" in the Scuola San Rocco, we can understand how the lines were drawn then with regard to the validity and sufficiency of static patterns of architectonic order. Both Panofsky and Wittkower make the mistake, I believe, of assuming that the classical architecture of Palladio, Serlio, and Vignola is that of progressive and enlightened humanism, in contrast to the Gothic of the Middle Ages. Their judgment is based, it would seem, on style alone, not on an examination of the position and the purposes of the institutions for which these rigorously correct buildings were designed. What was being countered by their imposing formalities was not medieval feudalism (it was the land-holding aristocracy, old and new, that commissioned the distinguished villa and chateau architecture of the sixteenth century, both in Italy and in France); the enemy was to be found among men such as Machiavelli, Copernicus, Calvin, and Peter Brueghel.

15. From Bertrand Russell's brief introduction to V. F. Calverton's *New Generation* (New York, 1930), a collection of essays by various writers, all dealing with children and the family. The book contains many extreme statements about the inadequacy and the iniquity of the institution of the family as it has traditionally functioned in Western civilization.

Wright was made especially sensitive to the problem of family relationships, as were also Butler and Strindberg, by the events of his own childhood. As he has explained in his *Autobiography,* his father was a preacher and a musician, a self-absorbed itinerant at heart, a chronically unsuccessful man who could find no place for himself in his world. His mother, on the other hand, had an intense feeling of family loyalty and responsibility, felt strong ties to the farming community near Spring Green, Wisconsin, from which she had come, and was deeply concerned with the education and the destinies of her three children. William Wright and Anna Lloyd-Jones were prompted to marry, one gathers, largely by their common enthusiasm for intellectual and educational ideals. At the time of their first meeting, in 1864, he was a widower with three children, the oldest no more than thirteen years old, and was earning a modest living as a lawyer, as commissioner of the Richland County Circuit Court, as a peripatetic Baptist preacher, and as superintendent of the local school district, wherein Anna Lloyd-Jones was employed as a teacher.[15] They were married in 1866, but though they lived together for nineteen years, the marriage seems not to have been a happy one. Between 1866 and 1878 they lived successively in McGregor, Iowa, in Pawtucket, Rhode Island, and in Weymouth, Massachusetts, whereafter they returned in Wisconsin. The breaking point was finally reached in 1885. As the story is told in Wright's *Autobiography,* "One day when the difficulties between father and mother had grown unbearable, the mother, having borne all she could—probably the father had borne all he could bear too—said quietly, 'Well, Mr. Wright . . . leave us. I will manage with the children. Go your way.' " And he did; he walked out the door and "never was seen again by his wife or his children. Judge Carpenter quietly dissolved the marriage contract." [16]

That is the version of the story that Mrs. Wright told her children and her grandchildren; but since her son Frank was eighteen years old at the time of his parents' divorce, he must surely have known that the story was untrue. In the mid-1960s Thomas S. Hines had the good

15a. For a fuller account of the life of Wright's parents, see: Robert C. Twombly, *Frank Lloyd Wright, an Interpretive Biography* (New York: Harper & Row, 1973).

16. *Autobiography,* pp. 50-51.

sense to consult the court records and brought to light the fact that it was William Cary Wright who had sued his wife for divorce, citing a list of grievances that ranged from her refusal to mend his clothing to her refusal of "intercourse as between husband and wife." Just why their son persisted in defending his mother's account of the event it is hard to say. Since the first edition of the *Autobiography* was published nine years after Mrs. Wright's death, it was not simply in order to spare her feelings. Plainly the emotional bond between mother and son was uncommonly strong—as also was the son's resentment, perhaps, toward his aloof and authoritarian father, even though the members of William Wright's various Baptist and Unitarian congregations seem always to have found him to be an admirable and engagingly attractive man. Perhaps it was our architect's misfortune to have been born at a time when the relation of masculinity to femininity was undergoing a searching reexamination; or perhaps it was just that childhood experience of extremes of loyal devotion and of individualistic detachment, of migrant insecurity and of rooted stability, of strong-willed but indulgent motherhood and of sensitive but exasperated and frustrated fatherhood, that prepared Wright for being the most deeply concerned and emotionally committed of modern domestic architects.

A Precarious Commitment

One day not long ago a well-known architect was asked by a well-meaning dowager, "Oh, Mr. So-and-so, you're a *modern* architect, aren't you?" To which the architect replied, "Madam, if I were a surgeon, would you ask me if I am a *modern* surgeon?" [17]

There is abroad today, especially in professional circles, a conception of the architect as a specialist in solving other people's problems, even as a doctor treats other people's ailments—a conception which puts the architect at the opposite pole from the musician and the abstract-expressionist painter, who are ostensibly preoccupied with experiences of self-expression or self-release. The idea obscures the fact that the architect's style may be shaped no less than other artists' by personal and emotional factors of a kind we do not in the least

17. Norman T. Newton, *An Approach to Design* (Cambridge, Mass.: Addison-Wesley Press, 1951), pp. 1-2.

associate with the surgeon's activity. While to architects of the common run such factors may not be especially important, they are obviously so to the first-rate architectural artist—and never more plainly than in Wright's case; for it is an inescapable corollary of his concern for the intimate institution of the family that the sources of his art were centered, as they are for the musician and the still life painter, in his self-awareness. One of the most conspicuously conservative aspects of his work and thought is that which bears upon the preservation of his image of himself.

PLATE I

The nature of that image is revealed most directly in the many portrait photographs Wright made and had made of himself throughout his life. He was intensely aware of his own appearance and, like Rembrandt, liked to strike poses that would reveal what he understood to be his nature. One recognizes immediately that the kind of self-characterization we see in these photographs has been extinct in modern painting since well before 1900. To find fully comparable images from the hand of a major artist we must go back to the time of Courbet or even Delacroix, beyond which the history of the type can be traced back to the early fifteenth century. Between 1425 and 1865 the point was reiterated in thousands of portraits that a man is a *character*: that he possesses a distinct and constant spiritual identity which determines and is determined by the role he plays on the world's stage, where "all the men and women are merely players." The conception of man as a character depends, that is, upon certain convictions concerning the significance of history, or of the succession of events experienced in time. These convictions took shape in the Renaissance and reflect the persuasion that there is an all-embracing destiny that gives high meaning to the course of a man's life, to his interactions with other people, and to the historical development of the state to which he and they belong. Until the advent of Impressionism both painters and musicians persistently affirmed that men participate with one another in a vital drama that has a purposeful beginning, that is led within an ordered and intelligible framework (in painting, a rational perspective; in music, the diatonic scale and a constant metrical pattern), and that leads inexorably toward a meaningful resolution and conclusion. Repeatedly it is avowed, as in the landscapes of Rembrandt and Ruisdael, Constable and Courbet, that the qualities of mood, pathos, and dramatic tension belong to the structure of the word itself, in the very nature of which the stage is set for the unfolding drama of human destiny.

It is to this conception of man that David Riesman refers when he speaks of the "inner-directed" man of earlier generations, in contrast to the "other-directed" man of the twentieth century. In his deep sense of personal destiny, in his faith in the power of an "organic Divinity" in the world, in his strong feelings about the relation of man to Nature, Wright revealed his complete devotion to that older image, both of man and of the world. "When I first worked for Dad," writes John Lloyd Wright, "I observed that he was convinced that a Source existed which, by its very nature, produced ideas in the mind that could be reproduced in the world. The rejection of his work by ignorance did not faze him. He concentrated on the intelligence that accepted it." [18] It was this faith that made it possible for him to be a "character" of that distinctive sort that, according to a number of recent observers, has almost disappeared from the American scene. What distinguished Wright from Erich Fromm's "market personality" or Riesman's "other-directed man" was his unshakable conviction that he *had* a role to play, a destiny to fulfill, even as had the prophets of the Old Testament or the signers of the Declaration of Independence. His eccentricities of dress and manner were of central importance to the definition of that role as he understood it; for it could not be played in the gray-flannel suit or with the stereotyped mien of the "organization man."

But now we must ask why anyone committed to this view of man's nature should have attempted to express it in terms of the relatively static and impersonal art of architecture. The view had always found its best expression in what Hegel regarded as the highest of the arts, painting, poetry, and music, and had been virtually ignored by the practitioners of the "symbolic" art of building. Why should Wright not have became a painter? Or a musician?

To answer such questions we must reflect again upon the character of architectural art. I have contended that it is conservative in nature, devoted to the defense of something that is bound up with the

18. John Lloyd Wright, *My Father Who Is on Earth* (New York: G. P. Putnam's Sons, 1946), p. 108.

state and its institutions. Let us consider in this connection the following passage from an article by the Harvard psychologist Jerome S. Bruner:

Our concern is with conceptions of man, with the forces and ideas that have given shape to our contemporary image of man. I need not insist upon the social, ethical, and political significance of this image for it is patent that the view one takes of man affects profoundly one's standard of the humanly possible. And it is in the light of such a standard that we establish our laws, set our aspirations for learning, and judge the fitness of a man's acts. It is no surprise, then, that those who govern must perforce be jealous guardians of man's ideas about man, for the structure of government rests upon an uneasy consensus about human nature and human wants. The idea of man is of the order of *res publica*, and by virtue of its public status the idea is not subject to change without public debate. The "behavioral scientist," as some people nowadays insist on calling him, may propose, but society at large disposes. Nor is the idea of man simply a matter of public concern. For man as an individual has a deep and emotional investment in his image of himself. If we have learned anything in the last half-century of psychology, it is that man has powerful and exquisite capacities for defending himself against violations of his cherished self-image. That is not to say that Western man has not persistently asked: "What is man that thou art mindful of him?" It is only that the question, when pressed, brings us to the edge of anxiety where inquiry is no longer free.[19]

Wright was not inclined by temperament, it would seem, toward asking radically original questions about the meaning of his experience—questions of the sort that had been and were being asked by Cézanne, Freud, Picasso, and Joyce—but rather was deeply anxious to defend, in an increasingly hostile or indifferent world, an image of man and an ethical standard he had been reared to believe in. It was in the nature of the image itself that his role should be prophetic and proclamatory, critical and iconoclastic; but this should not conceal from us its essentially defensive and conservative character. No doubt Wright was sufficiently perceptive to see that what was undermining the image he cherished had to do less with the actions or attitudes of individuals than with the larger ethical, socio-economic, religious, and

19. Jerome S. Bruner, "The Freudian Conception of Man and the Continuity of Nature," *Dædalus* (Winter 1958), 77; reprinted in *Science and the Modern Mind,* ed. Gerald Holton (Boston: Beacon Press, Inc., 1960).

political framework that had for centuries sustained a certain conception of meaningful individuality. In insisting that he wanted to create an *American* architecture, he made it plain that his concern was indeed with *res publica*; for without the support of a certain order of public things, without a certain setting of the institutional stage, his self-image could not be preserved. Set in the context of Taliesin or Fallingwater, that image seems wholly credible; put down in the Lake Shore Drive Apartments, it may seem almost ludicrously implausible and inflated.[20] One need not come dressed and prepared to play the part of Hamlet in a computer center; one needs the ramparts of a castle for that.

Wright's grandfather, father, and uncle were Unitarian preachers, and in their day the most influential spokesman for the philosophy of Unitarianism was Emerson. It was he who undertook to define the image of the distinctively American man that lies at the heart of Wright's understanding of selfhood and of human nature.

To believe your own thought, to believe that what is true for you in your private heart is true for all men,—that is genius. Speak your latent conviction, and it shall be the universal sense. . . . We but half express ourselves, and are ashamed of that divine idea which each of us represents. It may be safely trusted as proportionate and of good issues, so it be faithfully imparted, but God will not have his work made manifest by cowards. A man is relieved and gay when he has put his heart into his work and done his best; but what he has said and done otherwise shall give him no peace. . . . Society everywhere is in conspiracy against the manhood of its members. Society is a joint-stock company, in which the members agree, for the better securing of his bread to each shareholder, to surrender the liberty and culture of the eater. The virtue in most request is conformity. Self-reliance is its aversion. It loves not realities and creators, but names and customs.

Whoso would be a man, must be a nonconformist. He who would gather immortal palms must not be hindered by the name of goodness, but must explore if it be goodness. Nothing is at last sacred but the integrity

20. As early as 1924 Mies made the following assessment of the *Zeitgeist* to which he felt obliged to attune his architecture: "The individual is losing significance; his destiny is no longer what interests us. The decisive achievements in all fields are impersonal and their authors are for the most part unknown. They are part of the trend of our time toward anonymity." The Lake Shore Apartments were designed, one gathers, for the anonymous technician whom Mies regarded as the archetypal modern man.

> of your own mind. . . . Let us affront and reprimand the smooth mediocrity and squalid contentment of the times, and hurl in the face of custom and trade and office, the fact which is the upshot of all history, that there is a great responsible Thinker and Actor working wherever a man works; that a true man belongs to no other time and place, but in the centre of things. Where he is, there is nature. . . . But now we are a mob. Man does not stand in awe of man, nor is his genius admonished to stay at home, to put itself in communication with the internal ocean, but it goes abroad to beg a cup of water of the urns of other men. We must go alone. . . . I will so trust that what is deep is holy, that I will do strongly before the sun and moon whatever inly rejoices me and the heart appoints. . . . The populace think that your rejection of popular standards is a rejection of all standard. . . . But the law of conscience abides. . . . If any one imagines that this law is lax, let him keep its commandment one day.
>
> And truly it demands something godlike in him who has cast off the common motives of humanity and has ventured to trust himself for a taskmaster. High be his heart, faithful his will, clear his sight, that he may in good earnest be doctrine, society, law, to himself, that a simple purpose may be to him as strong as iron necessity is to others! . . . We want men and women who shall renovate life and our social state. . . .[21]

Line by line, these are the ideas Wright strove to live by. There runs through them a strong strain of idealism; for it is presupposed that any man who is "true to himself" will find himself in harmony with other honest men, since the individual's "latent conviction" is inspired by the "divine idea" and is thus identical with the "universal sense," in tune with nature itself.

In fact, however, the tension between the demand for self-reliant independence and the need for the collective values of "doctrine, society, law" posed difficult problems for both the philosopher and the architect. "We must go alone"; but it does not follow that by doing so we "shall renovate life and our social state." Indeed, the very idea of a society of nonconformists—an idea that is related to, but that goes well beyond, Renoir's conception of a Society of Irregularists—is paradoxical and impossible of realization. Toward the end of his life Wright confessed rather ruefully to one of his former apprentices that the one area in which he felt he had failed was that of human relationships. It was a consequence of his basic commitments that the intimate fellowship with which he deliberately surrounded himself in his later years

21. From Emerson's essay, *Self-Reliance,* 1841.

at Taliesin was something he often found hard to endure. To the extent that it truly was a fellowship, it threatened to diminish its leader and its members by promoting conformity. Even more paradoxical, of course, was the effort at defending Emersonian self-reliance in terms of the essentially collective and institutional art of architecture.

Wright accepted Emerson's ideas; yet the two men seem far apart in character. For the realization of the image of man to which Wright clung, one must turn to Whitman, in all his ebullient and joyous vigor—to the "Song of Myself" and the "Song of the Open Road" and the "Song of Joys" and the "Song of the Broad-Ax." In an anonymous review of his own *Leaves of Grass,* Whitman pictures himself and the ideal poet as a man who "steps into literature, talking like a man unaware that there ever was hitherto such a production as a book, or such a thing as a writer. . . . He must recreate poetry with the elements always at hand. He must imbue it with himself as he is." Here is the artist Wright sought to be: the man who strides into his profession with utter disdain for the profession itself, convinced that there never has been built a really satisfactory American building, that the very art of architecture must be recreated from the ground up, and that that the recreation must begin with a reconsideration of the building materials which are the "elements at hand." Above all, the architect must imbue his art with *himself.* "Most of the great poets," declared Whitman, "are impersonal. I am personal. . . . In my poems, all revolves round, concentrates in, radiates from myself. I have but one central figure, the general human personality typified in myself."

Meyer Schapiro has observed that a close relationship exists between Whitman's conception of the mobile, striding, purposeful, self-reliant writer and the image of the artist that Courbet (who was only eleven days younger than the American poet) set forth in his "Bonjour, M. Courbet." Even more apposite to our concern, perhaps, is the painter's sympathetic portrait of the Fourierist, Jean Journet, "partant pour la conquête de l'harmonie universelle," in that Wright, as the designer of Broadacre City, carried into the twentieth century a tradition of utopian planning in which the name of Fourier looms large. There comes to mind, too, the figure of Robert Owen, traveling up and down the world in pursuit of the just society that he thought it was his mission to inaugurate singlehandedly; and that "child of Free-

PLATE II

dom," Thomas Carlyle, speaking out with "Indignation and grim fire-eyed Defiance" against the devil and all his machinations.

One thinks of the importance of physical activity to both Whitman and Wright—of Whitman's frequent use of the word "athletic," of Wright's love of horseback riding, swimming, dancing, skating. "Afternoons after four o'clock I had been in the habit of riding Kano, my young black horse (named after the Japanese master), over the prairies north of Oak Park, sometimes letting him run wild as he loved to do, sometimes reining him in and reading from a book usually carried in my pocket, for I've always loved to read out-of-doors—especially Whitman." [22] It is not hard to find the lines he must have liked; they spring at us from almost every page.

Allons! with power, liberty, the earth, the elements,
Health, defiance, gayety, self-esteem, curiosity:
Allons! from all formules!
From your formules, O bat-eyed and materialistic priests.

O to realize space!
The plenteousness of all, that there are no bounds,
To emerge and be of the sky, of the sun and moon and flying clouds, as one with them. . . .

The main shapes arise!
Shapes of Democracy total, results of centuries,
Shapes ever projecting other shapes,
Shapes of turbulent manly cities,
Shapes of the friends and home-givers of the whole earth,
Shapes bracing the earth and braced with the whole earth.

"The art of art," wrote Whitman, "the glory of expression and the sunshine of the light of letters is simplicity. Nothing is better than simplicity. . . . To speak in literature with the perfect rectitude and insouciance of the movements of animals, and the unimpeachableness of the sentiment of trees in the woods and grass by the roadside, is the flawless triumph of art." [23] And Wright: "To know what to leave out and what to put in; just where and just how, ah, that is to have been educated in knowledge of SIMPLICITY—toward freedom of expres-

22. *Autobiography,* p. 162.
23. Walt Whitman, *Preface to Leaves of Grass,* 1855.

sion." [24] And as the first of the six propositions he set down for himself in 1894: "Simplicity and Repose are qualities that measure the true value of any work of art." [25] Both men's use of the word simplicity is an interesting one, for in structure neither the poetry of Whitman nor the architecture of Wright is at all simple. In fact, the Dutch architect Oud has averred that one of Wright's most obvious traits was his romantic love of *complexity*. However, neither Whitman nor Wright employs the word in a simply descriptive sense. For both it is essentially an ethical term, pointing to a way of life that is "simple" by virtue of being in harmony with the "simplicities" of nature, as against the pretentious complexities of civilized society. "Any wild flower," according to Wright, "is truly simple but double the same flower by cultivation and it ceases to be so. . . . Jesus wrote the supreme essay on simplicity in this, 'Consider the lilies of the field.' " [26] Wright's notion of simplicity has little or nothing to do with the aesthetics of the International Style—a point that has been obscured by the many writers who have sought to prove the homogeneity of the so-called Modern Movement. For Mies, as for the Le Corbusier of *Vers une architecture,* the perfect simplicity, it would seem, is that of the efficient machine. Theirs is an ideal which does not admit the possibility of ornamentation; but there is no incompatibility whatever between ornamentation and the simplicity of the lilies—for "Solomon in all his glory was not arrayed as one of these."

Because of the difficulty of relating their ethic to our modern society, Emerson, Whitman, and Wright shared an oddly dichotomous attitude toward the American republic. All three were enthusiastic about its promise and sharply critical of its achievements. For all three America was an inspiring ideal.

> The Americans of all nations, at any time on earth, [wrote Whitman] have probably the fullest poetical nature. The United States themselves are essentially the greatest poem. In the history of the earth hitherto the largest

24. *Autobiography,* p. 144 (typography of 1st edition, 1932).
25. "In the Cause of Architecture," 1908, p. 156.
26. Frank Lloyd Wright, *The Natural House* (New York: Horizon Press, 1954), p. 42.

and most stirring appear tame and orderly to their ampler largeness and stir. . . . Here is not a nation but a teeming nation of nations.

But he adds,

I say that our New World democracy, however great a success in uplifting the masses out of their sloughs, in materialistic development, products, and in a certain highly deceptive superficial popular intellectuality, is, so far, an almost complete failure in its social aspects, and in really grand religious, moral, literary, and aesthetic results. . . . I say that democracy can never prove itself beyond cavil, until it founds and luxuriantly grows its own forms of art, poems, schools, theology, displacing all that exists, or that has been produced anywhere in the past, under opposite influences. . . . Viewed, today, from a point of view sufficiently over-arching, the problem of humanity all over the civilized world is social and religious, and is to be finally met and treated by literature.[27]

Wright's confidence in the potentialities of America was likewise unlimited.

Opportunity to develop an architecture today lies with those sincere and direct people who, loving America for its own sake, live their own lives quietly in touch with its manifold beauties,—blessed by comprehension of the idea of freedom that founded this country. In our great United States notwithstanding alleged "rulers" or "benign" imported cultural influences, these spontaneous sons and daughters are the soul of our country; they are fresh unspoiled life and therefore they are your opportunity in art.[28]

Should our democracy now determine to build for the freedom peculiar to itself, our ideology could well serve for the emancipation of humanity. I believe this nation *will* so build.[29]

Like Whitman, Wright was persuaded that the diseases of humanity were to be healed by art, though by architecture rather than by literature. In a century when poets no longer espoused Whitman's image of man, which was related in some measure to the pioneering spirit of the 1840s and '50s, Wright clung to it tenaciously, even though he knew it was scarcely tenable in the nation America had become; for "we cannot have an organic architecture unless we achieve an organic society. . . . What can we do with an organic architecture in general as the

27. Whitman, *Democratic Vistas,* 1841.
28. Frank Lloyd Wright, *The Future of Architecture* (New York: Horizon Press, 1953), p. 208.
29. *Genius and Mobocracy,* p. 85.

architecture of a whole people so long as we have no whole people, but only a society so superficial as ours has become?"[30]

Which was to come first, the architecture that would emancipate a benighted and uncultured humanity, or the renovation of society that would make possible an organic architecture? Wright could never say. He declared to the end that we would have no culture of our own until we had an architecture of our own; but he insisted, also, that a society as chaotic as he believed ours to be cannot produce a great architecture. Like Emerson and Carlyle, he was profoundly concerned with the improvement of mankind's lot, with the perfection of the social state; but like them, too, he believed that that could be brought about only by the nonconforming, even *absolute* individualist. It was on the basis of this charged and precarious commitment that he had to invent his architectural forms.

30. *Future of Architecture,* p. 291.

TWO

WRIGHT AND ROMANTICISM

LONG BEFORE NOW THE READER HAS PROBABLY muttered to himself, "But is not all this only to say that Wright was a romantic? And hasn't everyone always known that?" Undoubtedly. He knew it and said so himself. Ever since the Middle Ages men have used words related to "romance" to designate whatever pertains to poetic sentiment, imaginative fantasy, the love of novelty and adventure; and it was this original sense of the word romantic that Wright knew to be applicable to his own volatile temperament. He would have rejected, however, any suggestion that he was a representative of the Romantic School or Movement. Perhaps it is in the very nature of his conviction that the romantic must think of himself as being a radical individualist, not as one who conforms to an established set of conventions—and certainly not as a *retardataire* conformist at that! Nor is it as such that I mean to picture Wright—though his relationship to that earlier movement is scarcely deniable.

Surely it is our most wretched inheritance from nineteenth-century historicism that even today, despite our reservations about historicist criticism, we find ourselves compelled to associate any given set of style-forming attitudes with a particular period of time and to believe that any expression of those attitudes may be regarded as vital and authentic only if it occurs within the limits of that style period—after which time it is only an example of *passéisme*. So it is that Romanticism is regarded as the legitimate expression of the spirit of the late eighteenth and early nineteenth century, whereafter it was succeeded by Realism, and that in turn by Impressionism, and so on. A full-blooded romantic of the mid twentieth century could never be regarded as a genuine modern artist, for Romanticism had already had its day a hundred years earlier. And yet the landscapes of Constable and the trios of Schubert seem to most of us as fresh and alive as if they had been created yesterday—more alive, in fact, than most of the painting and music of our own decade; wherefore, how can we say that what they affirm is dead and gone, not to be touched by a living artist?

How we define Wright's relationship to the Romantic period, and what we make of it, will depend upon what we take the nature of Romanticism to be. It goes without saying that the word has been defined, the movement characterized, in innumerable ways: by its enemies, as a lapse into irresponsible emotionalism, aimless egoism, anti-intellectual primitivism, amorality, and violence; by its defenders, as a renascence of wonder, a triumph of enthusiasm, the exaltation of poetic imagination. In fact, it was not without reason that Professor Lovejoy declared a generation ago, "The word 'romantic' has come to mean so many things that, by itself, it means nothing. It has ceased to perform the function of a verbal sign." [1] Yet even though it be the despair of the lexicographer, the word continues to be used, and used effectively, to point to a complex of attitudes with which we are all familiar.

Hebraism and Hellenism

I SHOULD like to propose, as a means toward gaining a better understanding of Wright's work, not a new definition but a new descriptive characterization of Romanticism. The word is associated in our minds with another which is loosely thought of as being its opposite—namely, Classicism. What I shall try to demonstrate is that these two attitudes or perspectives derive from the two main sources of Western thought, the Hebrew and the Greek respectively. Both strains are present in the thinking of all of us, as has been the case ever since the two were fused in an unstable amalgam during the first four or five centuries of Christianity.

For the most part my analysis is based upon Thorlief Boman's extraordinary book, *Hebrew Thought Compared with Greek*. "If Israelite thinking is to be characterized," writes Boman, "it is obvious first to call it dynamic, vigorous, passionate, and sometimes quite explosive in kind; correspondingly, Greek thinking is static, peaceful, moderate, and harmonious in kind." From the Greek point of view (which is the one Irving Babbitt takes toward Rousseau), "Hebrew thinking and its manner of expression appear exaggerated, immoderate, discordant, and in bad taste." [2]

The crux of the matter, as Boman sees it, lies in the difference between the Greek and Hebrew conceptions of being.

1. Arthur O. Lovejoy, "The Discrimination of Romanticisms," *Publications of the Modern Language Association,* XXXIX (1924), 232.

2. Thorlief Boman, *Hebrew Thought Compared with Greek* (London: SCM Press, 1960; Philadelphia: Westminster Press, 1961), p. 27.

The characteristic mark of *hayah,* in distinction from our verb "to be," is that it is a true verb with full verbal force. . . . Ratschow's attempt to understand the Old Testament's perception of reality from the concept of *hayah* is . . . a fortunate stroke. From *hayah* we can understand what "being" was consciously or unconsciously for the Israelite; "being" is not something objective as it is for us and particularly for the Greeks, a datum at rest in itself. . . . In the full Old Testament sense "being" is pre-eminently *personal being* (*Person-Sein*). What does it mean that a person *is*? If we try to define that by means of the concepts of impersonal and objective thought, we have to grasp for "becoming" as well as for "being" and still fall far short of the objective. The person, on the other hand, is in movement and activity, which encompasses "being" as well as "becoming" and "acting," i.e., he *lives*; an inner, outgoing, objectively demonstrable activity of the organs and of consciousness is characteristic of the person. Personal being is a being *sui generis* which is incommensurable with the "being of things (*dingliche Sein*), and therefore cannot be expressed in terms which are grounded in impersonal and objective things.[3]

The Greek conception of being was never more perfectly expressed than in the ordered architecture of the Greek temple. Static, lucid, wholly subject to rational and objective analysis, the orders are the quintessence of what Wright detested in traditional architecture, though he was never able clearly to say why he disliked them so. Sullivan had called them "feudal," which was patently ridiculous. What both men felt, we may be reasonably certain, was that the temple orders were a religious expression of a theory of being that they sensed to be alien and essentially blasphemous. No building better lends itself to sculptural adornment than does the Greek temple. It receives into its own anatomical structure and houses superbly within itself those impersonal body-objects which the Greek sculptors so loved to chisel out—objects that were expressly prohibited by the second commandment for the very reason that they tend to equate personal being with the being of things.

Our analysis of the Hebrew verbs that express standing, sitting, lying, etc., teaches us that motionless and fixed being is for the Hebrews a nonentity; it does not exist for them. Only "being" which stands in inner relation with something active and moving is a reality to them. . . . Thus, he dwells in a place who has alighted there or who can depart therefrom. . . . "Dwelling"

3. *Ibid.,* pp. 45-46.

for the Hebrews is related to the person who dwells, while for the Greeks and for us it is related to the residence and the household goods.[4]

In various figures of speech Wright avowed his determination to produce an "organic" architecture, a "living" architecture, an architecture imbued with the "order of Change"—but always the verbal metaphors were inadequate to convey his meaning, which had to do, it seems plain, with the Hebrew conception of the absolute primacy of personal being, the being of the person-who-dwells in contrast to that of the dwelling-as-object.

Boman's analysis of the Hebrew outlook illuminates another aspect of what has commonly been regarded as nineteenth-century romantic thought—i.e., the notion, often associated with the name of Gottfried Semper, that the design of a work of art or of craftsmanship is determined by or is latent "in the nature of materials" (a phrase of Wright's which Hitchcock chose as the title of his book on the architect, even though it has no bearing whatever upon his presentation of the buildings).

Our way of thinking is different from that of the Hebrews and Semites; we first of all conceive of the altar, i.e. its form, and then the material out of which it is made while presupposing that an altar formed and used in this way could as well have been made, e.g., of copper. For us, therefore, the form and the matter of anything are separate, and the form is the principal consideration; for the Semites the material is the thing. If an altar is wooden, then it could not possibly be copper, for that would result in a totally new and different altar, namely a copper one.[5]

Modern critics have sometimes berated the Greeks for producing, in the classic Doric temple, a "dishonest" imitation in stone of what had originally been an "honest" wooden building. Yet there is no reason to suppose that it mattered in the least to the Greeks whether a Doric column was made of wood or of limestone or of marble or of brick and stucco. Its meaning resided in its *form*. Wright, on the other hand, thought in Hebrew:

I began to study the nature of materials, learning to *see* them. I now learned to see brick as brick, to see wood as wood, and to see concrete or glass or

4. *Ibid.*, p. 31.
5. *Ibid.*, p. 37.

metal. See each for itself and all as themselves. Strange to say, this required greater concentration of imagination. Each material demanded different handling and had possibilities of use peculiar to its own nature. Appropriate designs for one material would not be appropriate at all for another material. At least, not in the light of this spiritual ideal of simplicity as *organic plasticity*. Of course, as I could see, there could be no organic architecture where the nature of materials was ignored or misunderstood. How could there be? Perfect correlation is the first principle of growth. Integration, or even the very word "organic" means that nothing is of value except as it is naturally related to the whole in the direction of some living purpose.[6]

Inseparably joined with Wright's attitude toward materials is his conception of architectural "functionalism"—one that he learned, broadly speaking, from Sullivan and which derives again from the Hebrew-romantic strain in our thinking.

In the entire Old Testament we do not find a single description of an objective "photographic" appearance. . . . Noah's ark is discussed in detail. . . . It is striking in this description that it is not the appearance of the ark that is described but its construction. What interests the Israelite, is how the ark was built and made. . . . The appearance is not directly alluded to by a single word. . . . The Israelite also when he confronts other objects such as buildings, is interested in them not for their appearance but first for their use; they are for him tools or implements of human or divine actions.[7]

The Greek architect is at his best in producing a Parthenon, which comes close to being an unused and *useless* building. Its value lies in its exemplification of an ideal of static harmony, of right measure and right relationship, of the goverance of *logos*; it was not conceived "in the direction of some living purpose." For Wright it was the utter antithesis of the organic.

6. *Autobiography,* p. 148. Needless to say, I do not mean to suggest, when I say that Wright "thought in Hebrew," that he had any knowledge of that language, or that he would have liked to acknowledge a debt to the traditions of Old Testament thought. For one thing, his writings are occasionally tinged with something that might now be called "anti-Semitism"—though it seems likely that his rather disdainful attitude toward Jews was merely an expression of the conventional and unreflected-upon stance of most midwestern Americans at the turn of the century. More importantly, Wright was so thoroughgoing a Romantic that he would have hated to think that his ways of thinking, far from being original and advanced, were extraordinarily old-fashioned!

7. Boman, *Hebrew Thought Compared with Greek,* pp. 74-76.

Let it be said at once, however, that not all modern functionalism is of this Hebraic genre. The ideal that was advanced by Sullivan and Wright was charged with poetic sentiment, as one learns as well from Sullivan's *Kindergarten Chats* as from Wright's *Testament.* In that section of the *Chats* in which Sullivan enunciates his celebrated but generally misunderstood dictum, "Form follows function," the examples he cites, it should be noted, are biological, not mechanical:

The form, oak-tree, resembles and expresses the purpose or function, oak; the form, pine tree, resembles and indicates the function, pine; the form, horse, resembles and is the logical output of the function, horse; . . . the form, full-blown rose, recites the poem, full-blown rose. . . . All, without fail, stand for relationships between the immaterial and the material, between the subjective and the objective—between the Infinite Spirit and the finite mind. . . . All is growth, all is decadence. Functions are born of functions, and in turn, give birth or death to others. Forms emerge from forms, and others arise or descend from these. All are related, interwoven, intermeshed, interconnected, interblended.[8]

Sullivan vehemently rejects the Greek conception of form, the beauty of which, as Boman observes,

lies in the plastic and consequently in the tranquil, moderate, and harmonious expression of the intellectual motive. . . . The Israelite finds the beautiful in that which lives and plays in excitement and rhythm, in charm and grace, but also and particularly in power and authority. It is not form and configuration which mediate the experience of beauty, as for the Greeks, but the sensations of light, color, voice, sound, tone, smell, and taste. . . .[9]

This is precisely the conception of beauty Sullivan has in mind when he writes:

All is function, all is form, but the fragrance of them is rhythm, the language of them is rhythm: for rhythm is the very wedding-march and ceremonial that quickens into song the unison of form and function, or the dirge of their farewell, as they move apart, and pass into the silent watches of that wondrous night we call the past. So goes the story on its endless way.[10]

8. Louis Sullivan, *Kindergarten Chats,* Section 12.
9. Boman, *op. cit.,* p. 87.
10. Sullivan, *Kindergarten Chats, loc. cit.*

Only in these terms can we understand the meaning of Sullivan's catch-phrase, "form follows function," of which the purport is not that the form of a building should logically be derived from, and only from, utilitarian and structural considerations, but rather that it should exuberantly proclaim, should radiantly show forth, the goodness of the human experiences which the use of the building will give rise to. Yet for all of his poetic insight, Sullivan's gift as an architectural designer was a curiously limited one. He had little or no feeling for the differences among materials: "to him all materials were only one material," Wright notes, "in which to weave the stuff of his dreams." The shapes of his buildings are for the most part stolid and inert. What they possess of the "fragrance of rhythm" is no more than skin deep: it is engendered mainly by that efflorescence of lilting ornament to the invention of which Sullivan devoted his best talents.

Wright preferred another phrase, "Form and function are one." Certainly this better expresses what Sullivan himself had had in mind, since it eliminates the misleading suggestion of causality or of logical derivation that is present in "Form follows function." Needless to say, their theory of function has nothing whatever to do with the problem-solving functionalism of the anonymous specialists of a firm such as Skidmore, Owings, and Merrill. An orientation toward problem-solving derives from Greek science, not from Hebrew poetry. Boman makes a useful distinction between the "logical thinking" which for the Greek was the highest form of intellectual activity, and the "psychological understanding" that was sought by the writers of the Bible.

> When we think logically we place ourselves objectively and impersonally outside the matter and ask what is the strict truth about it; when we would understand a matter psychologically, we familiarize ourselves with it and through sympathetic pursuit of its development we try to grasp it as a necessity.[11]

The conventional functionalist in present-day architectural practice thinks in Greek, one might say, while Sullivan and Wright thought

11. Boman, *Hebrew Thought Compared with Greek,* p. 141.

PLATE IV
PLATE III

in Hebrew.[12] What this means in terms of design can best be made clear by a comparison of two buildings, Wright's Price Tower and, say, Mies's Seagram Building. Whereas the latter is a wholly impersonal and objective statement about the possibilities of purity and perfection in design—the purity of an irreducibly simple system of construction and the perfection of a system of proportions—Wright's tower vigorously declares, by means of its rich variations of color, material, shape, saliency, and rhythm, its architect's conviction that life in the modern city —for the doctor and the engineer in their offices no less than for the family in its apartment (the Tower contains both offices and apartments) —should be lively and exciting, touched with novelty and adventure, rising high and proud in the midst of mundane banality.

It will be one of my purposes to demonstrate, then, that though the Bible has played an incalculably important role in shaping western thought for some two thousand years, it was only with Wright that Biblical thought found expression in the art of architecture, which has been dominated almost exclusively by the Greco-Roman tradition. There are obvious reasons why this should have been the case. Since the ancient Jews had had little in the way of visual art, it was inevitable that the early church, which kept alive the art of building for a thousand years after the fall of Rome, should have turned to Greek and Roman sources for its art and architecture. Although medieval Christendom had many of the characteristics of a Levantine society, its languages were Latin and Greek, not Hebrew, and its socio-political purposes were determined in large measure by its Roman heritage. Its

12. I do not mean to suggest that the measured and impersonal style of Mies and his imitators can be regarded as a modern equivalent of the traditional classicism that descends from the Greek temple. While it possesses something of the formal purity and objectivity of classic style, it quite lacks that relationship to the *word* which is essential to the humanizing significance of the ordered architecture of the past. Whereas every part of the Greek temple, from the smallest to the largest, has its own distinctive form, belongs to a class of similar and interchangeable parts, and can be identified by name, the Miesian building consists only of rectangles—shapes that have little relation to the human body and which do not come together, in a work such as the Seagram Building, to constitute a society of *members,* as do the parts of the Parthenon. Insofar as Greek may be regarded as the language of science (a development which could never have arisen on the basis of Hebrew thought), one may say that Mies's antecedents are Greek. However, he does not share the concerns of the Greek architect.

model Christian soon came to be the disciplined and obedient monk, living under the constitutional rule of a lawfully established Order; it could not risk the pursuit of what had seemed to the earliest saints and apostles to be the radical implications of Christ's teaching (as they are revealed, for instance, in the fourth chapter of the *Book of Acts*). Wright's thinking was essentially *protestant*; it was rooted in the Bible and stood relentlessly opposed to the analytical objectivity of what may generally be described, for want of a better word, as "Aristotelianism" in ethical, religious, and institutional matters.

The Paradox of Polarities

IN ORDER to understand the formal problems with which Wright wrestled, we must take into account not only the Hebraic background of romantic thought but also something of its characteristic shape and tendency. What most clearly distinguishes it from classic thought is its attraction toward just those poignant and vivid extremes of experience which Plato and Aristotle considered eccentric and excessive and urged the rational man to avoid. The romantic's experience is shaped by the tension between and among those attractions; he rejects the normative and medial tranquility which the classicist regards as the highest spiritual good.

The extremes toward which the romantic is drawn can best be understood not as eccentric departures from normality but rather as paired opposites or polarities. The archetypal romantic, surely, was Jean-Jacques Rousseau, who, in the years following his sudden illumination or conversion on the road to Vincennes, developed his mature philosophy around the polarity of personal liberty and social equality, or of freedom and justice. These are the problems to which he chiefly addressed himself in his two most influential books, *Emile* and *The Social Contract*. While a tension between opposites is implicit in these works, with their respective emphases upon the private and the public, the individual and the collective, Rousseau did not advance a theory or principle of polarity—though he was acquainted with the word.

His writings produced no surge of romantic enthusiasm in France, where the intellectual climate did not then favor the propagation of his ideas or of his image of man. It was rather among the younger generation of English and German writers that he found his most sympathetic audience; and it was one of the greatest of that generation, Goethe, who developed the idea of polarity as a general principle at work in the universe. Goethe pointed to the existence of many polar oppositions: active and passive, male and female, plus and minus, atomistic and dynamic, centripetal and centrifugal, analysis and synthesis, and, summing up all the rest, systole and diastole—that basic principle of contraction and expansion, attraction and repulsion, which, as he saw it, permeates the order of nature. "Das Geeinte zu entzweien, das Entzweite zu einigen, ist das Leben der Natur; dies ist die ewige Systole und Diastole, die ewige Synkrisis und Diakrisis, das Ein- und Ausatmen der Welt, in der wir leben, weben, und sind." [13]

Among English writers the most outspoken champion of Goethe and his works was Thomas Carlyle, for whom the German author was a "true Hero." It was due to his friendship with Carlyle that Emerson was inspired to purchase a fifty-five-volume set of Goethe's works and to immerse himself in the poet's writings. Although his enthusiasm was rather more guarded than his friend's, Emerson came to regard Goethe as being, along with Napoleon, one of the two great exponents of the civilization of the nineteenth century and to include him as the representative writer among his *Representative Men*. So it was that Goethe entered the mainstream of that current in American thought in which Wright was caught up; so that in 1949 the latter could list the names of ". . . Whitman, Emerson, Thoreau, Nietzsche, Goethe, Rousseau . . ." as chief among the modern exemplars of the tradition in which he knew himself to stand.[14]

Giuseppe Gabetti has characterized Romanticism in the following terms:

> Romanticism appears now as a revolutionary movement, now as a movement of restoration; now as a faith in the "bonté naturelle" of man in a state of nature and now as a mystical exaltation of cultural values; now as individualism and now as a religious sentiment concerning the unity of social life; now as subjectivism and now as the conscience of people, . . . now as an affirmation of the irrational forces of life and now as the triumph of the liberty of the spirit; now as dissatisfaction with reality and now as a

13. Goethe, *Farbenlehre*, Section 739.
14. *Genius and Mobocracy*, p. 57.

poetic transfiguration of that same reality; now as the poetry of melancholy, of sorrow, and of death and now as the discovery of a new and more intimate richness of existence; now as the victory of fantasy and of sentiment over reason and now as the conquest of a higher plane of rational life; now as a sentiment of "life as becoming"—in opposition to that sentiment of "life as being" which is so important to classicism—and now as an ecstatic religiosity in which all becoming flows again without distinction into the unity of "divine being"; now as an historicistic orientation and now as mystico-aesthetic idealism; now as a return to the Middle Ages and now as the foundation of modernity. . . .[15]

How many of these antitheses are exemplified in Wright's thought! He prided himself upon being a revolutionary trail blazer, responsible for the principal innovations that have determined the character of all modern architecture, but at the same time he regarded himself as the defender of a universal organic ideal whose nature has been misunderstood by virtually all modern architects. He had unbounded faith in the natural goodness of man, yet he was scornful of virtually all the products of human endeavor he saw in the world around him. He had only contempt for the institutions of Western civilization, but he had great confidence in the cultural promise of the United States of America—in spite of the fact that he repeatedly spoke of it as a cheap, commercialized, and barbarous mobocracy. He would have liked for there to be "as many kinds of houses as there are kinds of people," but he was deeply concerned lest social disunity should frustrate the cause of the new architecture, which was to be the architecture of a "whole people." He frequently hypostatized "Life" as an ultimate vitalistic value and spoke of architecture as a "Great Spirit," while at the same time he avowed his confidence in reason, common sense, and a "hard-as-nails" approach to social and architectural problems. He was greatly excited by the concept of Growth and welcomed the diversity that growth and change must bring, yet he looked forward to the day when "in this modern era Art, Science, and Religion—these three will unite and be one, unity achieved with organic architecture as center."[16] He espoused the cause of what he understood to be progressive modernity

15. Giuseppe Gabetti, "Romanticismo," *Enciclopedia Italiana,* XXX, 63.
16. Frank Lloyd Wright, *An Organic Architecture—the Architecture of Democracy* (London, 1939), p. viii.

in architecture (new materials, new uses of the machine, and so on), but the only social and architectural tradition for which he had unqualified admiration was that of feudal Japan. He was the champion of democracy and freedom, yet he was capable of being the most autocratic of men. He ceaselessly praised the virtues of loyalty, integrity, and simplicity, even while he was himself acting in ways that could only be described as disloyal, irresponsible, and extravagantly ostentatious. He dreamed of a day when every man would be "absolutely self-sufficient," yet at the same time he declared, both in his writings and in his buildings, that we are embraced by and involved within a pattern of relationships that is immeasurably larger than ourselves. In short, he was a thoroughgoing Romantic, oscillating between opposite positions with respect to all those matters with which he was most deeply concerned.

Architectural Music

THE ROMANTIC proclivity toward polarities was revealed throughout the nineteenth century in a way that is especially apposite to the study of Wright: namely, in the tension that was felt to exist between the arts of architecture and of music, the only arts in which Wright was seriously interested. Time and again one finds reiterated certain arguments for the primacy of one or the other. The matter was already actively debated in the first decade of the century. From the year 1805 comes Friedrich von Schlegel's pronouncement that "Architecture is the basis and groundwork of all other imitative arts, and no revival of art can take place until a grand improvement is seen in architectural design." To say that architecture is "the mother of the arts"—a favorite nineteenth-century notion to which Wright was unalterably committed—is to assert, in effect, that the significance of the arts is rooted in the cultural life of a society, that their reference is to a body of commonly cherished beliefs and patterns of relatedness, and that one of their principal purposes is the promotion of fellowship and understanding in the community (cf. Tolstoy's *What Is Art?*). It is to argue that the society precedes and brings into being the person, that the public takes precedence over the private.

From the beginning of the nineteenth century this conviction was associated with the idealization of the thirteenth century and of the Gothic cathedral, which has long been considered to be the exemplification *par excellence* of architecture as the mother art. This glorification of the Middle Ages exerted a powerful influence upon the Arts and Crafts Movement in the second half of the century and, through it, upon Wright, upon the Bauhaus, and upon the Modern Movement in general. Gropius's conception of "total architecture" grew directly out of this tradition. Just as his nineteenth-century predecessors had looked upon the cathedral as an expression of the "life" of medieval society and had generally ignored its relationship to the pressing particularities of an institutional and historical situation, involving the specific attitudes and ambitions of the leaders of the French church and of the French monarchy, so Gropius liked to envision the architecture of a "total society" in which institutional divisions, which reflect genuine differences of purpose and conviction, would have been quite eliminated.

At the opposite extreme there were those who rejected this view of the matter and proclaimed instead the supremacy of music among the arts. This was Hegel's position in part: he was persuaded that the progressive development of art had been from a lower stage in which architecture was predominant to a higher one which even then in his own lifetime was witnessing the ultimate triumph of poetry, painting, and especially music. Also from 1805 comes Schelling's assertion that architecture is "frozen music" (*erstarrte Musik*) and is susceptible of analysis in terms of such essentially musical concepts as rhythm and tonality. The idea had been partially anticipated in Goethe's early writings about Strassburg Cathedral; in 1829 he said to Eckermann, "I have found a paper of mine in which I call architecture frozen music. Really there is something in this; the tone of mind produced by architecture approaches the effect of music." Madame de Staël, whose response to German Romanticism was quick and sympathetic, spoke of architecture as "stationary music," and Nathaniel Hawthorne wrote in his *American Notebooks* (1839), "If cities were built by the sound of music, then some edifices would appear to be constructed by grave, solemn tones; others to have danced forth to light, fantastic airs." Behind all such statements lies a common desire—that of equating the experience of architecture with the experience of music, or of establishing a personal and dynamic basis, as against a public and institutional one, for the meaningfulness of buildings. Still in our own day this is the concern of those who, like Bruno Zevi, would have us believe that a building should be perceived as space rather than as substantial form. What Zevi implies is that only the temporal experience of the mobile observer has value; significance does not reside in the static patterns of structure as such.

The most uncompromising expression of the *pro musica* position is Pater's: he saw "all the arts in common aspiring towards the principle of music; music being the typical, or ideally consummate art, the object of the great *Anders-streben* of all art, of all that is artistic, or partakes of artistic qualities." [17] Denouncing as iniquitous the claims that system, idea, and convention make upon us, he insisted upon the ultimate privacy of the individual's experience.

> Experience, already reduced to a swarm of impressions, is ringed round for each one of us by that thick wall of personality through which no real voice has ever pierced on its way to us, or from us to that which we can only conjecture to be without. Every one of those impressions is the impression of the individual in his isolation, each mind keeping as a solitary prisoner its own dream of a world. Analysis goes a step farther still, and assures us that those impressions of the individual mind to which, for each one of us, experience dwindles down, are in perpetual flight; that each of them is limited by time, and that as time is infinitely divisible, each of them is infinitely, divisible also; all that is actual in it being a single moment, gone while we try to apprehend it, of which it may ever be more truly said that it has ceased to be than that it is.[18]

Herein lies the basis of Pater's conviction that music is the consummate art: it is the art that deals most intimately and most directly with what he regards as the very substance of our existence—"that continual vanishing away, that strange, perpetual weaving and unweaving of ourselves."

Whether or not a polar opposition necessarily exists between architecture and music is, of course, debatable. The two arts have been

17. Walter Pater, *The Renaissance* (London, 1873), from essay on Giorgione.

18. *Ibid.*, from the "Conclusion," written in 1868.

employed, in different places and at different times, for a variety of expressive and symbolic purposes, all of which cannot be covered by a single generalization. Nevertheless, it is easy to see what are the characteristics of the two that gave rise to a polaristic interpretation of them in the last century—in an era, that is, when men were much preoccupied both with the broadest aspects of cultural history and social theory and also with the subtlest forms of individual self-awareness. The two arts are alike in being nonrepresentational or "abstract," wherefore they lend themselves in some ways to comparison, as Schelling and Goethe perceived. But whereas music is the most insubstantial of the arts, being utterly without bulk, weight, location, or physical constancy, and without reference to anything possessing such attributes, architecture is the most substantial, manifesting itself always in huge, heavy objects with extraordinary powers of endurance. Music is an art of pure dynamics, in which every effect depends upon vibration, movement, and change (Wright often spoke of the Law of Change as something that would somehow have to be made to govern architectural design), while architecture is an art of pure statics, the very sense of which has always lain in its steadfastness. Where music has its being only in the momentary experience of performer and listener, and otherwise may scarcely be said to exist at all, works of architectural art are able to stand for centuries as unchanging landmarks, outlasting not only their builders but societies and whole civilizations, as well.

More important are the polar differences in metaphorical reference. Architecture is, in two senses of the word, the most essential of the arts: it is obviously associated with the basic necessities of human survival, and it serves as the primary symbol of those institutions by whose agency we are enabled to participate with one another as members of a common order or class or society. As expressive works of art, buildings pertain to what is held in common by generations of men in a given society; they are collecting in function and collective in meaning. Music, on the other hand, particularly in the form it has taken during the past three or four hundred years in the Western world, is the most existential of the arts. It is furthest removed from the word and the idea; it is an ordering of the successive moments of existence itself. It explores and articulates with infinite subtlety the qualitative variations of our vital awareness, but it makes no reference to anything that exists for us "objectively" in our world. It provides those occasions when we are most wholly absorbed, as William Kimmel puts it, in "the experience of experiencing." It embodies within itself and reveals to us most persuasively the dynamic kind of being that is expressed by the Hebrew verb *hayah* (v.s., p. 37).

No man was more perplexed by the relationship of music and architecture than Nietzsche. Music was associated in his mind with an infinite freedom of the spirit; yet the very freedom it expressed seemed to him a threat to the power and greatness he thought indispensable to a noble civilization and which he found best expressed in architecture.

The most powerful men have always inspired architects; the architect has always been under the suggestion of power. In the work of architecture, pride, triumph over weight, and will to power are intended to display themselves; architecture is a sort of eloquence of power embodied in forms. . . . The highest feeling of power and security is expressed in that which has the *grand style*.[19]

Yet Nietzsche could also speak of the *imposture* of the grand style and recognize clearly enough that the triumphant power he associated with buildings could entail—might inevitably entail—a loss of freedom. It is easy to see why Wright included Nietzsche in his list of spiritual forebears: to a great extent these are the problems with which he himself had to wrestle in trying to live the life of the romantic architect and to express his deepest convictions in architectural form.[19]

19. Nietzsche, *The Twilight of the Idols*, trans. A. Ludovici, Part 9, Section 11.

19a. It seems reasonably clear that the ambivalency Nietzsche felt with regard to the significance of buildings was part and parcel of the fabric of ancient Hebrew thought. From the brief account in the Book of Genesis we learn that Abraham left Ur of the Chaldees at God's command—that is to say, for what we would today call "religious reasons"—at a time that could not have been very many years after the completion of the great ziggurat of the moon-god Nannar in that city. Whether or not there was some connection between the erection of that idolatrous "Tower of Babel" and Abraham's departure we are not told, but in the light of the subsequent history of Israel it seems possible, at least, that there was. By a curious chain of circumstances, Abraham's great-grandson Joseph became a vizier of the pharaoh of Egypt, the land that had seen the invention of the "grand style" in architecture. Again there came God's command that his people leave, this time during the period that saw the building of the huge hypostyle halls at Luxor and Karnak by the powerful autocrats of the Nineteenth Dynasty. For some two hundred years or more after the death of Moses,

Havelock Ellis expresses the polarity in another way. "The art of dancing," he writes, "stands at the source of all the arts that express themselves first in the human person. The art of building, or architecture, is the beginning of all the arts that lie outside the person; and in the end they unite." [20] But do they in fact? Certainly the nineteenth-century Romantic was acutely aware of the tension between the subjective and the objective, between the self and the state, between freedom and convention, between dynamic inwardness and outer establishment. To assert, however, that the opposition is only apparent and that in the last analysis the tension must resolve itself in harmonious unity is at best an act of faith; we do not know that this must be the case.

It is just this faith that is avowed by Wright's favorite composer, Beethoven. Wright was convinced that no occidental architect had ever created structures that could match his own, but "when Beethoven made music I am sure he sometimes saw buildings like mine in character, whatever form they may have taken." [21] It is hard to imagine what formal connection Wright may have thought to exist between Beethoven's music and his own architecture, for musical and architectural structures are essentially incommensurable. Yet surely Beethoven expresses more effectively than any other composer that sense of dramatic destiny and of driving purpose, partaking at once of power and authority on the one hand and of exuberant personal freedom on the other, that was so central to Wright's conception of self and of creative activity.

his followers avoided both kingship and temple-building, those prime manifestations of "power and authority"; but eventually they succumbed and accepted Saul as king and Solomon as temple-builder. Pivotal in the history of Israel for the following thousand years were the successive destructions and rebuildings of the Temple, along with the railings of successive prophets against the arrogant sinfulness of cities that would surely bring down God's wrath upon the people. It is within that tradition of ambivalency that Wright himself wrestled with the ethics of architecture.

20. Havelock Ellis, *The Dance of Life* (Boston: Houghton Mifflin Company, 1923), p. 34.

21. *Autobiography*, p. 422.

From earliest childhood the two arts, music and architecture, must have been associated in his mind with conflicting attitudes and values. Even before his birth his mother had decided that she would have a son and that he would be an architect, to further which plan she hung woodcuts of English cathedrals in his bedroom. Later his musician-father taught the boy to play the viola and the piano and introduced him to the rudiments of musical theory. It seems not improbable that his parents' respective predilections in art were symptomatic of those differences of temperament and of purpose which led eventually to their divorce. It is in such polar tensions that we find our best clue, I believe, to the nature and meaning of Wright's work.

THREE

THE OAK PARK YEARS

WHEN THE YOUNG MR. WRIGHT STRODE onto the scene in Chicago, radiating the self-confidence of a giant-killer, he was not even dimly aware, it would seem, of the thorny problems he would have to contend with in creating an architectural expression of his Hebrew-romantic conviction. The measure of his naïveté can be taken from his *Work Song* of 1896.

I'll live as I work as I am
No work for fashion in sham
Nor to favor forsworn
Wear mask crest or thorn
My *work* as befitteth a man
My work
Work that befitteth the man.

I'll work as I think as I am
No thought in fashion for sham
Nor for fortune the jade
Serve vile gods-of-trade
My *thought* as becometh a man
My thought
Thought that becometh the man.

I'll think as I act as I am
No deed for fashion in sham
Nor for fame e'er man made
Sheath the naked white blade
My *act* as beseemeth a man
My act
The act that becometh the man.

I'll act as I'll die as I am
No slave of fashion or sham
Of my freedom proud
Hers shrive guard or shroud
My *life* as betideth a man
My life
Aye let come what betideth the man.

These verses reveal an extraordinary perceptiveness on their author's part, for in their ingenious welding of the notions of life-work-thought-deed-life, they set forth what is at the very heart of his concern. It was noted in the last chapter that the Parthenon superbly exemplifies the comprehensive meaning of the *word* for the Greeks. Behind romantic thought there lies not *logos* but the Hebrew conception of the word, *dabhar,* which is essentially different.

> *Dabhar* (word) is dynamic [says Boman] both objectively and linguistically. . . . The basic meaning is "to be behind and drive forward." . . . *Dabhar* means not only "word" but also "deed." The *word* is the highest and noblest function of man and is, for that reason, identical with his action. . . . The "deed" is the consequence of the basic meaning inhering in *dabhar*. . . . An Israelite would not therefore be able to burst out contemptuously like Hamlet, "Words, words, words!" for "word" is in itself not only sound and breath but a reality. Since the word is connected with its accomplishment, *dabhar* could be translated "effective word"; our term word is thus a poor translation of the Hebrew *dabhar,* because for us "word" never includes the deed within.[1]

To this Boman adds what is in the context of our purpose a most interesting observation, concerning "Goethe's translation of John 1:1: 'In the beginning was the deed.' Actually Goethe is on solid linguistic ground because he goes back to the Hebrew (Aramaic) original and translates its deepest meaning."[2] It is important to recognize, that is, that the Judeo-Christian or Biblical sources of romantic thought were matters of lively concern to the leaders of the romantic movement. Rousseau, who was a generation older than Goethe, had written, "I have loved the Gospel, I have adopted it, spread and interpreted it, I am attached to it with all the zeal of my heart. All my writings are imbued with the same love for the Gospel and the same veneration for Jesus Christ." Nothing in Biblical thought, perhaps, held so central an attraction for the romantic as did its dynamic conception of the word and of the indissoluble unity of word, deed, and self which is what Wright's *Work Song* is about.

And yet, when one stops to ponder the fact that the work it refers to was that of a fashionable suburban architect employed exclusively by prosperous businessmen (but not "vile gods-of-trade"?) and toward the end of gaining the wherewithal to live well and to make absurdly extravagant purchases of expensive clothing, furnishings, and *objets d'art* (but not for "fortune the jade")—by an architect who was

1. Boman, *Hebrew Thought Compared with Greek,* pp. 65-66.
2. *Ibid.*

greatly given to self-advertisement and was keenly aware of his place in his profession and in the cultivated social circle he served (but not of "fame e'er man made"?), then one has cause to wonder how any man could so thoroughly have misconceived the nature of his situation. Did he not realize that his early success depended heavily upon the *fashionableness* of Ruskin, Morris, and Arts and Crafts among the educated elite of suburban Chicago? Or that, as an architect, he could accomplish *nothing* except by appealing to the tastes of an established class and by working within the limits of the conventions that were acceptable to that class? It took Wright seventeen years to come to an understanding of such matters—but that is the subject of our next chapter.

Portrait Painting

I have described Wright's position as that of a man who was concerned equally and simultaneously for the extremes of independence and of membership, of change and of constancy, of spontaneity and of decorum, of originality of expression and of loyalty to a universal ideal; and I have observed that the ethical tensions which were generated by these polar attractions were for him bound up with, and could not be resolved apart from, the problem of the family and of the proper expression of its organizational principle. Already in his first years in Chicago he liked to design severely formal houses, such as Mr. Winslow's, and rambling, informal ones, such as his own cottage at Forest and Chicago in Oak Park.

If we were dealing with the work of a lesser architect—one who sought merely to please his clients rather than to express his convictions and to be "true to himself"—we might dismiss this apparent inconsistency as having been brought about simply by the personal tastes of his patrons; but although Wright professed concern for the character of each of his clients, he did not feel obliged to give them what they wanted. All of his houses reflect the style and thought of their creator as clearly as do the portraits of Rembrandt. The range of variation one sees among the latter's portraits of other persons corresponds to, or is even somewhat narrower than, the range one sees in his portraits of himself. So, too, with Wright; one feels that each commission presented him with an opportunity for solving afresh a problem that was essentially his own. When he drew up the list of his six "propositions" in 1894, he put first at the top of the page a quotation from Carlyle: "The Ideal is within thyself, thy condition is but the stuff thou art to shape that same Ideal out of." Or as Whitman had put it, "I have but one central figure, the general human personality typified in myself." Or Rousseau: "La bonté est donc l'adhérence immédiate et totale à soi. . . ." Wright's attitude toward his buildings, even after they were finished, was so proprietary that, long after taking possession, "his clients did not know whether the house was really theirs or his." [3] To the extent that a client made his house an expression of his own taste and of his own family's life and history, to that extent did he make it offensive to its architect. "Very few of the houses were anything but painful to me after the clients brought in their belongings." [4]

Wright himself drew an analogy between his role and that of a portrait painter. "Is a portrait, say by Sargent, any less a revelation of the character of the subject because it bears his stamp and is easily recognized by anyone as a Sargent?" [5] There are certain observations we need to make, however, with regard to the matter of the "architectural portrait." In the first place, it had long been felt among romantic artists that the art of portraiture was by its very nature one of indignity and compromise, prejudicial to the best interests of the true artist. As Geraldine Pelles has noted,

> Perhaps more than any other type, portrait painting subjected the artist to the specifications or vanity of his customers. . . . Many painters had a strong aversion to what they felt to be the indignities of such work. Blake refused to paint portraits at all. He left the protection of his patron Hayley who, he wrote to his brother James in 1803, "thinks to turn me into a Portrait Painter, as he did poor Romney, but this he nor all the devils in hell will never do. . . . I now defy the worst & fear not while I am true to myself which I will be." [6]

Miss Pelles might have added, if it had been germane to her purpose, that there is one art that surpasses portraiture in its subjection of the

3. John Lloyd Wright, *My Father Who Is on Earth,* p. 120.
4. *Autobiography,* p. 145.
5. "In the Cause of Architecture," 1908, p. 162.
6. Geraldine Pelles, *Art, Artists, and Society* (Englewood Cliffs, N. J.: Prentice-Hall, Inc., 1963), p. 31.

artist to the specifications of his customer—namely, architecture. While wanting, like Blake, to be "true to himself" above all, Wright was faced with an almost insurmountable difficulty by the very nature of the art he had chosen to devote himself to.

Secondly, it is not easy to say what the architect is making a likeness *of,* if he should consider his buildings to be analogous to portraits. In what way even a painted portait-image may be found to correspond to the nature or character of a living person is hard to specify. Traditional portraiture rests on the unspoken assumption, it would seem, that one can tell Hamlet from Rosencranz, Macbeth from Macduff, simply by looking at him; yet hardly anything in our experience of knowing people would seem to warrant that assumption—a point that Cézanne appears to have understood very well. But to think that any configuration of architectural elements might constitute a "portrait" of a living man or woman must surely seem farfetched. The stylistic variations that differentiate Wright's houses cannot, in fact, be clearly related to those qualities of temperament and predisposition that the words "personality" and "character" suggest to us, nor can we deduce by looking at those houses anything at all about the natures of their commissioners. Moreover, if Wright really believed, with Emerson, that "what is true for you in your private heart is true for all men," there would have been no reason for him to take serious account of the personal peculiarities of his clients, most of whom he probably could not have known at all well, anyway.

On the other hand, it is easy to see, as I suggested in the first chapter, that the very notion of our being "characters" lay at the core of what it was that Wright was trying to defend by means of the conservative art of architecture—and in that he was not alone, for similar things were being said on that subject at about the same time among the morbidly romantic artists of Vienna. At least one Viennese critic of the early 1900s imagined that he would approach his architect in the following way:

I should first have to tell an architect of my inner beauty—through my favorite color, poet, song, hour of the day. Then he would know me, would feel my very essence. He would have to express this through line. . . . Over the gate a verse would be inscribed: the verse of my essence: and what that verse is in words, all colors and all lines must also be; and every table, every wallpaper, every lamp would again be that same verse. In such a house I should see my own soul everywhere as in a mirror. . . . Here I could live of myself, looking at my own features and hearing my own music." (Hermann Bahr, *The Secession, Vienna, 1900,* p. 37, as quoted by Carl Schorske in *New York Review,* Dec. 11, 1975.)

The notion must have been current in Vienna for several years, for already in 1900 it had been mercilessly satirized by Adolf Loos in his "Story of a Poor Rich Man"—except that for him it is not the client who narcissistically demands that his personality be expressed, but rather it is the architect who insists upon designing everything in the house, including the client's bedroom slippers (to be worn in the bedroom only!), so as to produce an unalterable and imprisoning work of *Gesamtkunst* that the client ultimately finds unbearable. Loos knew something of Wright's work, of course, and may conceivably have had Wright in mind as well as the Secessionists whom he held in disdain. However, it was not until some years later, so far as we know, that Wright actually did go so far as to design, for the Coonley's in 1907/08, not only the furniture for their house but also the carpets, table linens, and even some of Mrs. Coonley's dresses, so as to envelop the life of the family in a totally harmonious *ensemble.* Whether or not it was because of Wright's tyrannical aestheticism that the Coonley's abandoned the house after only about three years we do not know—though we do know that they did not ask Wright to design another house for them when they moved to Washington (where Mrs. Coonley died in the 1950s).

What the notion of the "architectural portrait" leaves out of account altogether is the fact that a house is not built for a single person but for a family group, the members of which will not possess the same traits of character and will themselves change with the passage of time. If the house is well built, furthermore, it may be expected to stand for decades, even for centuries, so that it must be taken for granted from the outset that the building will change hands, hence should not be shaped to suit the idiosyncrasies of a single "personality."

The difficulty, as Wright came to understand rather slowly, lies in the fact that architectural forms relate not to the matter of personal character but to "a matter of government . . . a matter of the framework of a society;—the constitution of a civilization." The concern of the architect is inevitably with *res publica*—with the visible fabric of the city and with the enduring institutions of which it is composed. Yet if that is the case, what is the relevance of the assertion, "The Ideal is within thyself"? I think it fair to say that Wright was inclined to confuse two related yet separate ideas—that of individual personality with the broader and more diffuse notion of "personal being" that lies at the center of Biblical and romantic ontology. His deepest purpose was not to "express" this or that client's individuality, but rather to devise an architectural image or "icon" of the family-as-institution that would do justice both to the single member's claim to personal freedom and to the group's demand for mutuality and participation, while relating both freedom and participation to the rhythmic, vital, on-going *life* of the family.

But how? We find Wright oscillating in this early period between two conceptions of the family as the nuclear social group: on the one hand he wanted to establish its integrity and to insist upon the interdependence of its members—a concern that led him to stress the oneness of the sheltering roof, the centrality of the family hearth, and the simple regularity of the whole; while on the other, he sought, both in architectural imagery and in the conduct of his own life, to assert the independence of the individual—a desire that was expressed in broken roofs, irregular silhouettes, and highly variable groupings of architectural components.

The evidence suggests that during his Oak Park years Wright did not recognize the existence of this polar opposition. He appears to have maintained, until 1909, a naïve and optimistic faith in the feasibility of resolving the tension between individual and society within the context of the legal institutions and social conventions of the American suburb. One would think from reading his first article "In the Cause of Architecture" that there is no serious obstacle to an immediate realization of a new social and architectural order of things. The sense of the essay as a whole transpires in the following passage:

> This is the modern opportunity—to make of a building, together with its equipment, appurtenances and environment, an entity which shall constitute a complete work of art, and a work of art more valuable to society as a whole than has before existed because discordant conditions endured for centuries are smoothed away; everyday life here finds an expression

germane to its daily existence; an idealization of the common need sure to be uplifting and helpful in the same sense that pure air to breathe is better than air poisoned with noxious gases.[7]

Here was something as fresh and wholesome as Chautauqua itself, or as East Aurora and Arts and Crafts—the promise of a new life that would be simple, frank, sensible, sincere. Characteristically, Wright does not specify the "discordant conditions" which are to be smoothed away by the new architecture. One gathers, however, that he does not refer to conditions arising out of broad social and economic injustices or inequities in the American state, but rather to those that involve the organization and conduct of the middle-class suburban family.

In this same article Wright divides his houses into three groups according to roof type—hip, gable, and slab. His reason for doing this is not clear, unless it is simply to show that there is order and consistency in his work; for he draws no conclusions from his classification and has nothing to say about the special character of any of the three types. Rather than attempting to set up a typological system of this sort, we would do better, I believe, to interpret Wright's early houses with reference to the polarities discussed above. In order to show the constancy of these polar limits, let us compare two pairs of houses: the Winslow and Ingalls residences, of 1893 and 1909 respectively, mark the limit of formal symmetry and regularity, while the architect's own house and the Robie house, again some sixteen years apart, lie at the opposite end of the scale. In the first pair the architect has established unmistakably the oneness of the house-shape, the dominance of the central axis with reference to which every part is assigned to its place, and the sheltering spread of the single roof beneath which the house is closely contained. In the other two he has created a variable and unpredictable silhouette, has avoided obvious axiality, has broken the wall structure into planes of various sizes, has assembled those planes so that the pattern of joints seems broken and irregular, and has composed the roof of elements that are differentiated in size, shape, level, and directional axis. In the first pair a close relationship is maintained between the shape of the whole and the shape of the parts, while the parts themselves appear to be relatively few in number and

PLATE V
PLATE VI
PLATE VII
PLATE VIII

7. "In the Cause of Architecture," 1908, p. 162.

similar in size and form. In the second pair, on the other hand, the shape of the whole bears little resemblance to that of the individual parts, and the number and variety of the parts is conspicuously greater. In the first two the architect appears to have begun with an over-all conception of the whole, to which all the details are subordinated; while in the other two it is suggested, at least, that the whole was built up through the process of making many limited, *ad hoc* decisions and adjustments. The Winslow house seems to consist of a sequence of "frames within frames," whereas the Robie house looks as if it were made up of "blocks stacked upon blocks."

The Wright House: Work and Play

YET NONE of these four houses consistently exemplifies either polar extreme; within each one there are elements of formality and of informality. Initially the architect's own house on Forest Avenue was a rather conventional gable-roofed, shingled cottage. It was begun at a time when Wright was not yet deeply involved in domesticity and when his thoughts about the house and the family had not, it would seem, gone much beyond those of Silsbee. Soon after the cottage was finished, however, his family began to grow, and as it grew the house was gradually transformed into the rambling, irregular structure one sees today. At the same time there took shape the spontaneous and exuberant pattern of family life which, as John Lloyd Wright informs us, seemed to become the house so well.

> Horizontal lines; double-leveled rooms of one and two stories; scattered vases filled with leaves and wild flowers, massive fireplaces seemed to be everywhere. Here and there a Yourdes of rare beauty covered the floor. A Persian lantern, samovars, windows which met and turned the corners, lights filtering through fret-sawed ceiling grilles, sunshine and shadows . . . these made the house that was our home.
>
> A woven fabric of brown creosoted cedar shingles was studded with diamond-leaded glass. Massive common brick walls were enriched by stone urns and Boston ivy. Covered screened porches overlooked terraced gardens, a pool and fountain in a garden court. All this grew naturally out of the luxuriant landscape. . . .
>
> Papa's parties were best of all. He had clambakes, tea parties in his studio, cotillions in the large drafting room; gay affairs about the blazing logs that snapped and crackled in the big fireplace. From week to week,

month to month, our home was a round of parties. There were parties somewhere all of the time and everywhere some of the time. Bowls of apples and nuts, great jars of wild flowers were everywhere. . . .

No words, however true they would be, could do justice to the mischief in his eyes, nor to the humor he could pack away in a single gesture or facial expression. It was fun just to have him about.[8]

It was an intimate, casual little house, full of unexpected breaks and projections and without the least suggestion of dignified formality —except in one detail which attracts our attention because of its apparently incongruous relationship to the rest of the building. That one departure is to be found in the large playroom that Wright built when his oldest boys were still very young. In view of his avowed concern for smallness of scale, one might have supposed that the playroom would have been a low, open, casual structure; but in fact it was the largest and most formal room in the house, a high, barrel-ceilinged hall with a great fireplace at one end.

Certainly the playroom's size (big enough for twenty children, his son John says) bears witness to the architect's enthusiasm for childhood and for the kindergarten, but this alone would scarcely account for its almost baronial character. In seeking at least some tentative explanation of its form, we must go back, I believe, to Wright's own childhood. In his *Autobiography* he mentions three childhood experiences that may well bear upon the inspiration of the playroom. The first has to do with his attendance at an apparently exclusive school in Weymouth. "His mother's son has been in Miss Williams' private school for some years, no doubt with the usual Snobbyists and Goodyites. For several years, the minister's son was kept in this fashionable school with the few little Lord Fauntleroys Weymouth afforded." [9] He confesses that he cared little for and remembers little about that episode in his education; its emptiness stands in contrast to the richness of another learning experience that was begun at about the same time —the course of Froebelian kindergarten training that his mother brought back to Weymouth from the Philadelphia Exposition of 1876. With it came the Gifts, the beautiful blocks and pieces of colored cardboard with which he and his sisters played at a low mahogany table

8. John Lloyd Wright, *My Father Who Is on Earth,* pp. 15, 53, and 88.
9. *Autobiography,* p. 14.

under their mother's supervision. "And the exciting cardboard shapes with pure scarlet face—such scarlet! Smooth triangular shapes, white-back and edges, cut into rhomboids with which to make designs on the flat table top. What shapes they made naturally if only one would let them!" [10] Soon, however, the family returned to Wisconsin, the boy's golden curls were cut, and he was sent, at the age of eleven, to work on his Uncle James's farm. "And so the boy went. He went from Mother, books, music and city boys and father and little Maginel and Jane, idle dreams and city streets to learn to add 'tired' to 'tired' and add it again —and add it yet again. Then beginning all over again at the beginning, he learned to add it all up some more until it seemed to him he would surely break and drop." [11]

In his later years Wright was to become the champion of "ruralism," in opposition to CIAM's Urbanism, and was to preach "the unpopular gospel of Work." However, I believe we can best understand his early period in Chicago and Oak Park as a time of rebellion against the years of want and drudgery and obscurity he had known as a child, and a quest after those pleasures and advantages he associated with the city—books, music, the comforts of home, idle dreams, playmates. Later in his life he would associate different values with the city; but in the 1890s it was immensely important to him that his own children should have luxuries and time for play. "He took no personal interest," John Lloyd Wright reports, "in my religious or academic training. But when it came to luxuries and play, he tenderly took my hand and led the way." [12] Or as the architect himself says:

> So long as we had the luxuries, the necessities could pretty well take care of themselves so far as we were concerned. Season tickets to the Symphony; the children always tastefully dressed, in expensive things, the best that could be had. . . . This love of beautiful things–rugs, books, prints or anything made by art or craft or building–especially building–kept the butcher, the baker, and the landlord always waiting. Sometimes waiting an incredibly long time. Our kind grocer, down at the corner, Mr. Gotsch, came around once, I remember, with a grocery bill for eight hundred and

10. *Ibid.*
11. *Ibid.*, p. 18.
12. John Lloyd Wright, *op. cit.*, p. 26.

fifty dollars. . . . But the group of children big and little in the little gabled house on the corner with the queer studio alongside had unusual luxuries. Unusual advantages in education.[13]

In the light of all this we may perhaps understand the meaning the playroom had to its architect. In its imposing formality it is related to the class of Wright's buildings that pertain, as we shall see, to the city; but at this point in his life one of the important meanings the city had for him bore upon freedom, play, and an almost childlike irresponsibility. (That unpaid grocery bill would have amounted, in terms of today's money, to something in the neighborhood of ten thousand dollars!) Hence there is a certain logic or consistency in his having avoided the slightest trace of formal pretentiousness in every other part of the house and in having introduced this single manorial touch at just the point where the life of the family was most informal.

Soon after he had added the playroom on the south side of his house Wright made another and more important addition on the north —namely, the Studio. He had begun his practice in 1893 by opening a conventional office in the Schiller Building in downtown Chicago, but after two years he moved to combine his professional with his family life, if not under the same roof, at least on the same lot. It was then that he began to attract to himself the first of those enthusiastic young helpers or apprentices whose presence was to be a characteristic feature of his practice for the rest of his life. *Liebermeister* Sullivan had employed fifty draughtsmen, for whom he generally had undisguised contempt. ("Wright! I have no respect at all for a draughtsman!") But Wright, with his greater concern for the problem of human relationship, could never have assumed this attitude toward his employees. Both in Oak Park and later at Taliesin he felt it necessary that they should be drawn into and amalgamated with the life of his family. Although at Forest and Chicago the assistants could not live on the premises, as they later would at Taliesin, they formed a quasi-familial group of devoted followers who imitated, insofar as they could, their master's eccentric mode of dress and coiffure. Wright expected their relationship to him to be marked by loyalty and a devotion to certain ideas. They were taken on as members, not as hirelings. They were not mem-

13. *Autobiography,* pp. 118-19.

bers of his family, but they belonged to his household—an entity that had somehow to embrace within its pattern of order all that was socially meaningful.

We are not surprised, then, to find that the design of the Studio is one of the most interesting of Wright's inventions during that first decade of his practice. It involves both his family and his profession and is intended to show how the latter, with its public and communal implications, may be merged harmoniously with the former, which is intimate and private.

Winslow House: The Sacramental Home

On turning to the Winslow house we are struck first, as we have already seen, with its classic simplicity and proportionality. We recall that it was built in the year of the Columbian Exposition and are mindful (as its architect probably was not) of its relationship to the new taste for dignified restraint and formality that the Exposition would tend to promote throughout the country. As we contemplate its design we are especially impressed with the importance of the various binding and defining elements: the white frames around the windows, the broad white panel that contains the entrance, the salient white molding between the floors, the band of brown terracotta that is wrapped like a belt about the upper story, and the wide eaves that, when seen from below, appear to form a heavy white frame about the block of the house itself, paralleling the white molding that encloses the foundations underneath.

Yet for all its geometricality, the house seems to possess an extraordinary freshness and vitality, much as it did some seventy years ago when it "burst upon the view of that provincial suburb like the Prima Vera in full bloom." What chiefly lends excitement to the building is its color. By constructing the walls of warm yellow-buff brick and by placing a band of cocoa terracotta beneath the wide eaves, the architect has created the illusion that the house stands in a perpetual burst of bright sunshine that leaves a shadow around the upper walls and highlights the projecting moldings. Almost as important is the variation in material. The contrast between the surface textures of the flat Roman brick and the richly molded tiles makes for a kind of optical excitement that is quite lacking from the many "modern" houses that have recently been built on the same street. Moreover, the proportions of the Winslow house are novel and appealing: the building seems surprisingly close to the ground, partly because it is not perched on the kind of basement podium that was fashionable then and partly because, by raising the central molding, which seems to divide the floors, to the level of the second floor windows, Wright has made it seem that the roof has been brought down much further over the second story than is actually the case. The result is an appearance of intimate containment. "At this time I saw a house, primarily, as livable interior space under ample shelter. I liked the sense of shelter in the look of a building. I still like it." [14]

In connection with the Winslow house, which embodies one of Wright's most conservative statements about the family, it is interesting to consider something of the history of the theory of that institution in the Christian West. At the beginning of the Middle Ages St. Augustine "made selections from the writings of St. Paul and set forth a theory of the family which he thought would cure the ills of society. His three fundamental tenets were *fides* (loyalty), *proles* (children), and *sacramentum* (indissoluble unity of man and wife). His was essentially a domestic family concept." [15] Later, when marriage and the family came under the jurisdiction of canon law, the sacramental nature of marriage was reaffirmed despite the rather negative or equivocal attitude of the medieval church toward sexuality. The Protestant reformers of the sixteenth century generally denied that marriage is a sacrament and favored a secularization of the bond. Luther, however, "idealized the humble home, with father, mother, and children carrying on their daily duties. In his sermon *von ehelichen Stand* of 1529 he appeared to consider marriage almost a sacrament instituted by God, the most dignified of all the conditions of man. . . . He recognized that from the standpoint of religion marriage has a high value and put it above virginity and continence. Marriage is *the* religious state, he held." [16] With the rise of the atomistic family in the nineteenth cen-

14. *Ibid.,* p. 142.

15. Carle C. Zimmerman, *Family and Civilization* (New York: D. Van Nostrand Co., Inc., 1947), pp. 462-63.

16. *Ibid.,* p. 513

tury, the factor of *sacramentum* all but disappeared from the popular non-Catholic view of the institution of marriage; and as the size of the average family shrank and childless marriages became more common (as had been the case with the atomistic family in ancient Rome, also) *proles* lost much of the significance it had had for the Protestant reformers. This left only *fides* as the basis and support of the institution of marriage.

In 1909, Wright was to embrace this latter conception and to argue that when marriage ceases to be mutual, when it is no longer a matter of *consent,* in the fullest sense of the word, it becomes a form of slavery and should, as a matter of simple justice, be dissolved and set aside. At that time, after having begotten six children whom he loved and who loved him, he repudiated *proles,* as well. "After he left home Dad said he was not suited to be a father—never wanted to be a father—didn't feel right in fatherhood. He didn't say we weren't his children, but referred to us as 'their mother's children.' Children were not in his reckoning, he said." [17] But in designing the Winslow house in 1893, he set forth a very different conviction—an interpretation of marriage and the family which more nearly approximates Luther's than that of the "active family negationists" of his own day, such as Goodsell and Folsom.

It is particularly in the design of the reception hall that Wright affirms the sacredness of home and hearth. The room seems hardly to have been designed for family use; it is simply an entrance hall and a connecting space between the living room on the right and the library on the left. Yet it is the most formal, the most carefully articulated room in the house. Behind a delicate wooden arcade, which carries with it something of the sense or flavor of a rood screen before an altar, there lies a brick-walled alcove in the center of which is a broad, square-cut fireplace—large for this period, when most fireplaces were designed for coal grates. It is hard to imagine the area's being used for the ordinary activities of daily life; it looks as if it were intended for the celebration of some solemn family ritual, affirming the sacramental nature of the institution of marriage.

PLATE IX

17. John Lloyd Wright, *My Father Who Is on Earth,* p. 55.

The Winslow house is related in another way to Wright's concern at this time for the sanctity of the family.

During the winter nights of eighteen ninety-six and seven, Dad and Mr. Winslow worked on the magnificent book, *The House Beautiful.* They printed by hand, on handmade paper, 12 x 14 inches, ninety copies of this matchless book in the basement of Mr. Winslow's River Forest home—then gave them to their friends. Dad designed the setting and drew the intricate pattern freehand with pen and ink. William C. Gannett wrote the text. . . . To have put so much thought, energy and time into a work that frames so glorious an exposition on home, speaks clearly of my father's inner feeling in relation to his home and family.[18]

Gannett's text begins with the following words: "There is a Bible verse that reads, 'A building of God, a house not made with hands.' Paul meant the spiritual body in which, he says, the soul will live hereafter, but how well the words describe the home,—a home right here on earth!" And at the end of the first chapter:

"I heard a voice out of heaven," says another Bible verse,—"A great voice out of heaven, 'Behold, the tabernacle of God is with man, and He will dwell with them, and they shall be His people.'" Call the great power "God" or by what name we will, that power dwells with us in so literal a fashion that every stone and rafter, every table, spoon and paper scrap, bears stamp and signature to eyes that read aright: "The house in which we live is a building of God, a house not made with hands."[19]

This is precisely the attitude that is expressed, I believe, in the Winslow façade and in the reception hall. Perhaps the idea was initially Mr. Winslow's, but there can be no doubt about the fact that Wright was wholly in sympathy with it at this point in his career.

PLATE X

Only half of the character of the Winslow house is revealed in the street façade, however. Just as important as its formality is the informality of the opposite side of the house, which is broken into a variety of planes at different levels in depth, involves a complicated interplay among rectangular, curving, and polygonal shapes, and is dominated by the off-center stair turret to the same extent as is the other side by

18. *Ibid.,* pp. 42-43.
19. *Ibid.,* pp. 155-57. (The complete text of *House Beautiful* is reprinted in this book.)

the central doorway and chimney. The building confronts the city in one way, the garden in another—a matter I shall come back to in my final chapter.

Family As Form and Freedom

THE HOUSES Wright designed between 1893 and 1909 can be distributed along a line that runs, as it were, from the front of the Winslow house to the back. Closest to the pole of formal regularity lie the first project for Mrs. David Devin's house (1896), and the Thomas P. Hardy house (Racine, 1905). Not far from this extreme lie the George Barton house (Buffalo, 1903), the Stephen M. B. Hunt house (La Grange, Ill., 1907), and the Robert Evans house (Chicago, 1908).

PLATE XII
PLATE XI

Nearest the opposite pole we can place the W. A. Glasner house (Glencoe, Ill., 1905), the Frank Baker house (Wilmette, Ill., 1909), and the Isabel Roberts house (Riverside, 1908). Toward this end of the scale lie the Joseph Husser house (Chicago, 1899), the first *Ladies Home Journal* house (1901), and the W. E. Martin house (Oak Park, 1903) . Intermediate between the two poles lie such works as the Susan Dana house (Springfield, Ill., 1903) and the Arthur Heurtley house (Oak Park, 1902). In the former a number of heavy and rather formal components have been grouped together into a rambling complex, while in the latter a simple rectangular block has been subdivided into many lesser elements that vary in size, shape, color, material, and saliency. Of these many parts only the roof (but not the great chimney) is aligned with the axis of the plan.

One discovers in studying the interiors of these early houses that the polar contrast we have been discussing is manifested again and again in the dissimilar treatment of the dining rooms and the living rooms: the former tend to be as regular as the Winslow façade, the latter as irregular as the Glasner house. It is interesting to see what Wright himself has to say in this connection.

> Soon I found it difficult, anyway, to make some of the furniture in the abstract. That is, to design it as architecture and make it human at the same time–fit for human use. I have been black and blue in some spot, somewhere, almost all my life from too intimate contact with my own early furniture. Human beings must group, sit or recline, confound them, and they

must dine—but dining is much easier to manage and always a great artistic opportunity. Arrangements for the informality of sitting in comfort singly or in groups still belonging in disarray to the scheme as a whole: *that* is a matter difficult to accomplish. But it can be done now and should be done, because only those attributes of human comfort and convenience should be in order which belong to the whole in this modern integrated sense.[20]

As Wright perceived, the occasions of dining and of "living" give rise to quite different modes of grouping. At no time do the members of a family exhibit a greater oneness of purpose than in sitting down together for a meal. In his early houses Wright often treated the occasion almost as if it were liturgical in nature; his severely (and uncomfortably) rectilinear furniture, set squarely within a rectilinear architectural context, made these dining rooms seem more like stately council chambers than like gathering places for the kind of informal family life we usually associate with Wright's name. Like his rigorously symmetrical façades, they were conceived, it would seem, in the image of the state—that is to say, in terms of a patterning that Wright unmistakably associated with the established conventions and legal institutions of the city. They declare unequivocally that "architecture is the mother art"—that the unity of the group requires submission and conformity on the part of its members.[20]

PLATE XIV

In the living room, however, the family is not grouped with reference to a single and definable purpose. Occasionally it may be so, but ordinarily the relation of its members to one another is variable

PLATE XV

20. *Autobiography,* p. 145.

20a. Robert Twombly takes me to task, not without reason, for having ignored the relation of American turn-of-the-century dining rooms to the formal dinner party, which was governed by conventions that prescribed a kind of decorous orderliness that has all but disappeared from the social life of our present era of cocktail parties and informal buffets. He proposes, that is, that the polarity between dining room and living room derived from the conventional manners of Wright's clients rather than from the emotional and philosophical perturbations of his own mind. Twombly cites in this connection Leonard K. Eaton's interesting study of Wright's patrons in comparison with those of Howard Van Doren Shaw, a friend and contemporary of Wright's who designed "conventional" houses on the North Shore for a somewhat better-educated and more prosperous clientele than Wright ordinarily attracted—one to which the formal party was even more important, in all likelihood, than it was to Wright's clients in Oak Park. Yet in none of Shaw's mansions do we find the kind of polar opposition that is so striking in Wright's prairie houses. Instead, the two kinds of room possess very nearly the same qualities of sedately dignified casualness.

and unpredictable. Wright confessed that it was difficult to express this kind of connectedness in terms of an architectural scheme, since what was called for was a composition that achieved wholeness out of "disarray." The problem in this case is analogous to that of the still life painter, who must make an intelligible and integrated group with assorted objects that have no fixed or necessary relationship to one another, in contrast to that of the designer of a cathedral façade or of a fifteenth-century *sacra conversazione.* (Indeed, the association of an informal figure group with still life is a fairly common theme in European painting from the sixteenth century onward.)

Wright did not hesitate to say that the dining room was "always a great artistic opportunity," but it is plain that he felt a certain uneasiness about the order of disarray that the living room seemed to require; for such an order is intrinsically nonarchitectonic, if not antiarchitectural. Nevertheless, the problem one knows to have been genuinely compelling for him was not the easy task of creating formal and symmetrical patterns but the difficult one of reconciling order with freedom. In such works as the Baker, Roberts, and Robie houses he went as far as he he could, within the limits of the prairie-house formula, toward infusing a "living room" looseness into the shape and design of the house as a whole.

Wright often said, in his later years, that he designed all his houses "from the space within" or "from within outwards." Both phrases reveal his commitment to Rousseau's theory of personal development, as set forth in *Emile* (and in countless treatises by others on what eventually came to be called "progressive education): to wit, that the child should be allowed to develop even as a plant grows, unfolding from within so as to "fulfil the potentialities" that are inherent within him from the moment of conception; wherefore it is appropriate that favorable conditions should be provided for stimulating the child's development, but that he should not be forced into some "preconceived" pattern, lest one try to force a rose to look like a lily. But though one may, on the basis of this theory, generate a free and open kind of interior design, as Wright liked to do, one cannot so easily derive therefrom an exterior form that will show how the family takes its stand within the civilizing context of the community—that will indicate how civilization can "take the natural man and fit him for his place in this great piece of architecture we call the social state." Just as Rousseau never makes it clear to us that Emile's education is going to prepare him to live in the city that is described in *The Social Contract,* so Wright could never resolve the conflict between living room and dining room, or between interior and exterior—between what "arises from within" and what must be made to conform to the established standards or patterns of the community at large, apart from which we should scarcely be able to communicate with one another.

City Buildings

DURING THE period we have been discussing, Wright produced a moderate number of buildings for institutions other than the private family. The list includes the River Forest Golf Club, the Yahara Boat Club, the Francis Apartments, the Village Bank project, the Luxfer Prism Office Building project, the Abraham Lincoln Center projects, Unity Temple, the Larkin Building, the City National Bank and Hotel in Mason City, the River Forest Tennis Club, the Frank L. Smith Bank, the Warren McArthur Apartment project, and the Lexington Terraces project. All of these are essentially public buildings, and all of them are perfectly symmetrical in design. They all lie, that is, at the Winslow-façade end of our polar scale, and often they are articulated with geometrical patterns that closely resemble those of the Robie dining room. Wright was completely consistent in this. Whatever pertained to the life of the city outside and apart from the private family was expressed in terms of geometrical formality.

The one nonresidential undertaking of this period which has something of the rambling irregularity of the Dana and Baker houses is the Hillside Home School group, which Wright designed in 1902. That this should be the case only points up the architect's consistency, for that unique institution, which was operated by the architect's maiden aunts and to which his older boys were sent, was a home in a full sense of the word. Its character has been lovingly described by Mary Ellen Chase, who taught at Hillside for three years.

> It combined a farm, a school, and a home. This trinity of indivisible interests was in every sense a unity . . . When I think of Hillside and give back to it the appreciation of many years, I think of it, first of all, at its meal-

times. Then all its features of the best and wisest of homes were apparent. . . . Our meals at Hillside were the most pleasant of occasions. There was nothing whatever about them that savored of an institution, even of a school. The family atmosphere banished any other idea.[21]

These, then, were the terms and the limits within which Wright worked for seventeen years. At one extreme we find a formal and geometrical mode of relatedness which the architect associated with the city and with institutional order, with stability and with the submission of parts to a clearly defined whole; and at the other, a casual and irregular mode which connoted personal freedom and the repudiation of institutional conformity. While his public buildings all lie at the formal end of the scale, his private homes are distributed from one end of the scale to the other, with respect both to the whole design and to the ordering of individual rooms and lesser details.

Prints, Drawings, and Japan

AN INTERESTING subject that has been largely ignored in architectural criticism is the style of the perspective renderings of the various major architects. What is the character and quality of these drawings simply as works of graphic art? One cannot understand Le Corbusier's architecture, I believe, without taking into account the attitudes and presuppositions that underlie his taste on the one hand for sweeping vistas rendered in the tightest kind of linear perspective, and, on the other, for impulsive, scrawly little sketches which possess the characteristics of a highly personal signature.

For his part, Wright preferred an intimate and proximate presentation, so drawn that qualities of fastidious touch and of two-dimensional abstraction are emphasized. The manner suggests that a spacious openness exists around and in front of the building but not, as in Le Corbusier's renderings, behind and beyond it. The house is made to appear at once embraced within its natural setting and open to it. Often the rendering causes the house to look larger than it actually is; but at the same time Wright may choose to mitigate or even to obliterate entirely the formal symmetry of a structure, emphasizing instead

21. Mary Ellen Chase, *A Goodly Fellowship* (New York: The Macmillan Company, 1939), Chapter 4.

the freedom of perspective standpoint that belongs to the observer and, by implication, to the members of the household the building is designed to shelter. Such drawings illuminate the complexities of Wright's own attitude toward his houses as institutional symbols; they reveal to us the quality of his vision as nothing else can.

Perhaps a word should be said at this point concerning the much-discussed "Japanese influence" in Wright's work, for a number of his drawings are based, as he readily acknowledged, on the style of Japanese prints and screens. Wright repeatedly insisted that he had known nothing of Japanese architecture, other than what he could see in the prints, prior to his first visit to Japan in 1905. I find no reason to quarrel with his account of the matter; for the most striking connections one can point to are to be found, not between Wright's houses and the Japanese house, in all its Mondrianesque simplicity, but rather between his architecture and the style and structure of the Japanese print. (Compare, for instance, the accompanying print by Buncho with Wright's design for the living room of the Heurtley house.)

PLATE XIII
PLATE XV

To fully understand the issues involved in this relationship, however, one would have to undertake a three-pronged inquiry that lies beyond the scope of this treatise. In the first place, one would have to explore the relation of the prints to the changing cultural milieu of Japan two hundred years ago. In that country no less than elsewhere, the art of architecture was an extremely conservative one, preserving traditional forms that had been handed down with little change for many centuries. The eighteenth- and nineteenth-century prints, on the other hand, with their new iconography based upon domestic genre, the theatre, and a novel kind of landscape that emphasizes the perspective experience of the observer, reveal to us the rapid changes that were then taking place in the Japanese world, largely because of Western influence.

Having studied the implications of the new subject matter and new modes of composition, one would then have to consider the meaning of these same works to the generation of Western artists that was in its ascendancy at the time of Wright's birth—the generation of Manet, Degas, and Whistler, all of whom were delighted by the Japanese print.

It was their taste that supplanted the earthy "realism" of Courbet; they were contemporaries of William Morris and of the flowering of Arts and Crafts in England.

Finally, one would have to explore the intricacies and ambiguities of Wright's relationship to both the Japanese and the later Western episodes. Just as it is hard for us to associate the elegance and refinement of Utamaro and Whistler with the taste of Courbet, so, too, is it hard for us to associate them with Carlyle, Emerson, and Whitman. Were Wright's purposes related to those of the print-makers, in their break with the conservative Samurai aristocracy, or to those of Whistler, in *his* break with the American generation Wright so admired? There can be no doubt about the fact that Wright thoroughly enjoyed playing the part of the artist-esthete, as that part had been conceived by the contemporaries of Whistler, and that by becoming a collector of Japanese prints he gained access to a circle of cultivated devotees and connoisseurs that would otherwise have been closed to him—and gained it at a relatively modest price, in comparison with what it would have cost him to become a collector of Old Masters. The very fact that Japanese art and architecture seemed to lie quite outside the classical and humanistic traditions of the West made it possible for him to become an expert enthusiast without placing in jeopardy his own position as a defender of the newly-arrived businessman—the man who had won a place for himself by his own efforts and without benefit of ancestral tradition, even as had Wright's own grandfather, who had repudiated his place as a lowly artisan in class-conscious Great Britain and had made a new beginning for himself as an independent and self-reliant farmer on the Wisconsin frontier. And yet the role and social position that Wright was shaping out for himself could scarcely have been more different from his grandfather's—a circumstance that may well have some bearing upon the crisis in his career that loomed just ahead.

FOUR
CRISIS

IN THE LATTER PART OF 1908 AND THE FIRST months of 1909 a crisis was reached in Wright's career. He himself described it under the heading "The Closed Road."

> This absorbing, consuming phase of my experience as an architect ended about 1909. I had almost reached my fortieth year. Weary, I was losing grip on my work and even my interest in it. Every day of every week and far into the night of nearly every day, Sunday included, I had "added tired to tired" and added it again and yet again as I had been trained to do by Uncle James on the farm as a boy. Continuously thrilled by the effort but now it seemed to leave me up against a dead wall. I could see no way out. Because I did not know what I wanted I wanted to go away. . . . Everything, personal and otherwise, bore down heavily upon me. Domesticity most of all. What I wanted I did not know. I loved my children. I loved my home. A true home is the finest ideal of man, and yet—well, to gain freedom I asked for a divorce.[1]

After a period of waiting, the divorce was denied; whereupon Wright abandoned his practice and his family and fled.

Why did he flee? Hitchcock, in his account of the development of Wright's architecture (*In the Nature of Materials*), all but ignores the episode, implying that it was a personal matter that had little bearing upon the architect's career. Manson suggests that other persons were to blame—Mrs. Wright and especially Mrs. Harold McCormick. He is persuaded that if the architect's design for the McCormick house in Lake Forest had been accepted, Wright would have been

> placed in the vanguard of successful American architects, as the apostle of a new architecture to which the most serious attention must be given. It would have done more: it would have placed the stamp of social approval on the whole progressive movement in Chicago and extended its scope immeasurably. It might have turned the tide of eclecticism. The rejection of the design marks a pivotal point in the history of a trend toward modern design in America which, as it was, went down in *débacle,* not to rise again until the late 1920s.[2]

Mrs. McCormick was apparently responsible for rejecting Wright's scheme and for choosing, instead, an Italian villa which, Manson avers,

1. *Autobiography,* pp. 162-63.
2. Grant Manson, *Frank Lloyd Wright to 1910: the First Golden Age* (New York: Reinhold Publishing Corp., 1958), p. 202.

was erected on the ruins of the Chicago School. . . . Wright undoubtedly evaluated the McCormick fiasco at its true significance: the requiem for a whole school of architecture which had had the will and ability to make the United States the instigator of an architectural revolution that was long heralded and that could not, in any case, be indefinitely postponed.[3]

I find it hard to believe that the new architecture of Chicago rested upon such frail foundations that it could be brought to ruin by the rejection of a single project, or that Wright was so sensitive as all that to what others might think of his work. I am puzzled, too, by the idea that any kind of architecture should be considered revolutionary—or on the other hand, that any revolution should either require or deserve the "social approval" of the very rich. By 1909 Wright had built scores of houses for families of impeccable social standing and had been accorded both local and national recognition such as no architect in his thirties had received before or has received since. In 1908 the *Architectural Record* (which is published in New York, not in Chicago) had devoted an entire issue to the presentation of his first essay, together with no less than eighty-seven illustrations of his work—an issue in which even the advertisements for plumbing and heating equipment were illustrated with photographs of his buildings. In his own short bibliography Manson lists fifteen periodical references to articles by or about Wright from the years between 1900 and 1910. The notion that he fled because he had been rejected or ignored is manifestly untenable.

Manson further pictures Wright as being harassed at this time by financial worries, disaffection among his colleagues and assistants, and dissension within his household. But of these, only the household dissension was new; being deeply in debt was his normal condition, as was being at odds with his fellow architects. If such difficulties were aggravated now, it was almost certainly the result rather than the cause of Wright's uneasy state of mind at this point of crisis.

Let us put aside the popular image of Wright as a hurt and sensitive genius, driven by the indifference of his countrymen into the arms of appreciative foreigners, and begin our search for understanding with Wright's frank confession that he was losing interest in doing the kind of work to which he had devoted himself unstintingly for so many

3. *Ibid.*, pp. 202 and 211.

years. That work "had done something" to him which caused everything to weigh heavily upon him—"domesticity most of all," even though he knew himself to be primarily a domestic architect. But why?

Community Architecture

Knowing that any answer must be tentative, since we cannot grasp the whole content of Wright's experience at that time, I should like to advance the thesis that what closed the road was his dawning realization that he had failed. For seventeen years he had wrestled with the problem of resolving the polar tension between the personal and the institutional, between freedom and loyalty, between the individual and the state, between music and architecture; and during that time he had invented many different forms, always in an effort at finding an adequate expression of that resolution in the public art of building. But had he succeeded at any single point? He could design a harmonious room, but when his clients moved in with their possessions it was painfully apparent to him that they were not really in harmony with it—that simply by being their separate selves they were defacing a work of art that had ostensibly been made for them but that was in fact designed to set forth an ideal they did not fully understand or accept. He could design a subtly balanced and harmonious exterior, such as that of the Robie house, but there it stood on its narrow city lot, soon to be surrounded by houses that had nothing in common with it, so that instead of contributing to an image of urban harmony it seemed simply eccentric and incongruous—the interior situation turned inside out.

The problem lies deeper even than this. Wright's apologists assert that his work was not accepted as widely as it deserved to be. But let us suppose that he had been commissioned to build every house in Oak Park, and that the Winslow, Williams, Husser, Devin, Roberts, Hickox, Gale, Dana, and Robie houses all stood along a single street. Would they compose a better street than do the conventional houses of which Oak Park is mainly made up? Or even as good a one? "There should be as many kinds (styles) of houses," he wrote in 1908, "as there are kinds (styles) of people and as many differentiations as there are different individuals." Within the limitations of his own style Wright seems to have made an effort at observing this precept; but in so doing he had ruled out the possibility of achieving an orderliness in the larger community commensurate with the orderliness of each individual house. Yet that larger pattern was of the greatest importance to him, as an expression of the *res publica* with which he was ultimately concerned.

By 1909 Wright must have come to realize, verbally or not, that it is in the very nature of the city (and especially of the American city, with its strong pressure toward the maintenance of neighborhood homogeneity) that it enforces conformity, or is even in essence an expression of the idea of conformity. That is its shape, pattern, and meaning. Wright knew this; he liked the idea; and yet he could not fit the houses of free individuals into such a pattern. Somewhere there was a flaw in his conception of architecture. It had been there from the beginning, but it was only in developing his projects of 1907-09 that he was forced at last to confront the fact squarely. I have in mind specifically the Como Orchards community plan and the McCormick house.

The residences Wright designed in the 1890s—Blossom, Charnley, Parker, Harlan, Winslow, Bagley, Devin, Moore, Husser, and so on—are the most highly differentiated of all his works. Around 1900 he began to feel the need for greater uniformity of style and developed what Manson rightly calls the "formula" of the Prairie house, in terms of which most of his designs in the following decade were conceived. From the year of its inception, we discover, he was preoccupied with the idea of grouping together into a larger unit several identical houses of this type. The upshot was the Quadruple Block plan—a scheme with which he was actively concerned for the next ten or fifteen years and with which he tinkered from time to time for the rest of his life. Manson professes to see in it a solution to the problem of "placing the maximum number of individual dwellings on an average city block with maximum light and greenery." [4] Since there is no evidence that this was Wright's concern, and since these three maxima are mutually exclusive, it seems likely that Manson has invented a problem which, in the nature of things, does not really exist.

PLATE XVI

It is not demonstrable, indeed, that Wright's purpose was a practical one at all. Though the Quadruple Block was exhibited in Chicago

4. *Ibid.*, p. 207.

as early as 1902, it attracted no backers. The architect never found either four families who wanted identical dwellings (it was inconceivable, according to his own first principles, that such could be the case!) or a real estate investor who could believe that a series of such blocks would constitute a salable commodity. For these are not, after all, inexpensive row houses designed for mass production; they are substantial dwellings on half-acre plots (assuming that the block in question is three hundred feet square, as is more or less standard in middle-western America). A population density of four families to a block is characteristic only of expensive residential suburbs; but members of the classes that live in such suburbs are precisely the ones who resist most strongly the notion of uniform housing—and for reasons that Wright understood perfectly well and was himself in sympathy with.

Some years ago Manson published an ingenious and illuminating study of the relationship between Wright's prairie-house compositions and the block-construction diagrams that were part of the Froebelian kindergarten training in which he had taken such delight when he was about nine years old.[5] There is reason to believe, as Manson contends, that this early experience in composing structures of block-like simplicity out of simple blocks was a factor of some consequence in shaping the architect's style. We have already observed, however, that there was a measure of ambiguity in Wright's use of the block, in that he was inclined sometimes to regard it as a whole, sometimes as a part. On the one hand, as in the Heurtley design, he might consider the house to be a single block, and on the other, as in the Robie house, as a stack of blocks which is not itself block-shaped. These two possibilities are exploited in a variety of ways in the Oak Park period, but neither appears to have been found altogether satisfactory.

Now it seems to have struck the architect around 1901 that a larger and more comprehensive basis of unification might possibly be found in the block-pattern of the city itself. In later years he liked to say that he saw the low-lying, rectilinear form of the prairie house as being bound to and expressive of the "horizontal line of the prairie."

5. Grant Manson, "Wright in the Nursery," *Architectural Review,* CXIII (June 1953), 349.

In practice, however, he found that the type was as well adapted to mountainous sites as to flat ones (witness the Norman Guthrie project for Sewanee, Tennessee, and the prairie houses at Como Orchards); for in the closely built-up and tree-filled suburbs of the typical American city at the turn of the century the shape of the larger landscape, be it flat or hilly, was scarcely visible. It was rather, I believe, the rectangular grid of the city itself that was the essential factor in determining the new formula within which Wright worked between 1902 and 1909. Although there was little or no likelihood that he would ever be given an opportunity to design a whole block or series of blocks, he was nevertheless concerned from the outset with the significance of the block as a communal or collective unit, and as a form with which the open and rambling house of the free individual could be brought into harmony.

Wright's perspective rendering of the Quadruple Block inspires in us the conviction that the four houses, joined by walls that define a shady inner yard that is apparently held in common (the block itself has an interior and an exterior), are occupied by families that are in some way closely related to one another—by blood ties, perhaps, or by their connection with a business firm or their membership in a special club. It is implied, that is, that what binds them together is charged with emotional significance, that they are genuinely made members with one another in a group that is larger than the private family and is at the same time spacious and unconfining. They are bound together by the city itself—or at least by the neighborhood; for Wright was concerned with the city only in its relation to domesticity, not to commerce and industry.

Nor was Como Orchards a city in a full sense of the word. Here Wright was asked to design a complete colony of summer residences for a specific site in the Bitter Root Mountains of Montana. The project was initiated by a group of professors from the University of Chicago who intended to develop the colony both as a vacation retreat for themselves and as an economic investment in rental property. As the architect pictured it in 1909, the community would have consisted of fifty-three separate cottages around a great lodge where all the families were to have their meals together. It was to have been a family of fam-

PLATE XVII

ilies—a purely residential colony in which all the family groups would have assembled at mealtime, just as do the members of a single family at home.

Manson expresses surprise at the formality of the arrangement. "Taken as a whole, the plan seems arbitrary and rigid for a wilderness site, there is no feeling for the roughness of terrain, and the cottages to the rear of the lodge are inexplicably close toegther, as if land were at a premium." [6] But this is to judge the matter from a standpoint that Wright himself was to define only at a much later date and on the basis of presuppositions of which he was but dimly conscious, it would seem, in the 1900s. As late as 1909 he had at his disposal only one means of expressing in architectural imagery the idea of collective agreement—i.e., the kind of geometrical formality one sees in the Winslow façade, the Robie dining room, and Unity Temple. In order for Como Orchards to appear to *be* a community, it had to be composed, Wright felt, according to a simple and immediately comprehensible diagram; for the community's power to comprehend—to gather its members into a society—is avowed in the comprehensibility of its architectural scheme.

The Como plan is subtler and more interesting, however, than that of the Quadruple Block. One cannot easily tell from the perspective drawing the number of variations Wright worked upon the simple one-story prairie house of which the colony is composed, but apparently it is not greater than four, perhaps five at the most. These variations are prompted by considerations of size and possibly of site, but not of character. The full range of architectural shapes is set forth in the lodge, which is the nucleus of the community and the parent building from which all the others seem to have been derived. The mathematical or numerical basis of collectivity (something we ordinarily associate more with Greek architecture than with Wright's) was never more clearly affirmed: the houses are placed in groups of two, three, four, and five, and these groups can be seen as belonging to larger configurations of six, eight, ten, twelve, and so on. All the groups are distributed with reference to the axes of the symmetrical lodge.

Como Orchards presumably represents the best town plan that

6. Manson, *Frank Lloyd Wright to 1910,* p. 207.

Wright was capable of envisioning in 1909. But what of his belief that there should be as many kinds of houses as there are kinds of individuals? The town is made up of only one kind of house, as was necessitated by its architect's conception of a communal image. But would it not do violence to the individualities of two hundred or so persons who were to inhabit the town to ask them to accept as suitable housing these buildings of barracks-like uniformity?

"A More Populous House" and A More Stately Mansion

HOW WRIGHT would have answered such a question we do not know. But during this same period when his image of the ideal community was crystallizing into this kind of all-inclusive schematic pattern, his image of the ideal private house was taking quite another shape and finding expression in the Coonley house and the McCormick project.

PLATE XVIII

In Mr. Avery Coonley the architect found, or attracted to himself, a new kind of client. Though personally of rather nondescript character and attainment, he was heir to a fortune that provided him with an "independence," the like of which our society has not often seen since the passage of the income tax amendment. The connection between personal freedom and financial affluence is one that Wright had long been aware of. To live extravagantly, as if it were not in the least necessary to budget and to economize in order to meet one's obligations to others, had seemed requisite to the proper expression of his own freedom. For Wright it was a quixotic gesture; but he must have recognized clearly enough that Mr. Coonley—and Mr. McCormick, and later Henry Ford as well, who approached Wright in 1909—did in all truth enjoy, in that last heyday of immense private wealth, a freedom from petty obligation and restriction for which even the term "princely" is not altogether adequate. That men of this kind should have sought Wright out reveals a great deal about both him and them. They had excellent reason to do so, but it was hardly because he was "the most progressive architect in practice," as Manson would have us believe. This is not to say that he was the most conservative, but simply that neither term, encumbered with its present connotations, rightly describes the situation.

His new patrons did not have to settle, as had Wright himself and his earlier clients, for two or three building lots on a suburban street. In 1906 Mr. Coonley had acquired a tract of several acres in Riverside, and in the following year, as well as can be ascertained, he and his wife (the decision was probably hers) gave Wright virtually *carte blanche* to design as fine a house as he could for them and their one child, Elizabeth, who was then about eight years old. For this family of three the architect produced what Manson aptly describes as the palace of the prairie houses. Within the limits of this relatively small suburban tract (a long oval, the greater part of which has recently been subdivided and studded with small houses), Wright managed to create the semblance of a splendid private estate, complete with stable, cow shed, chicken yard, shop, paddock, gardener's cottage, spacious walled gardens, and an extensive wooded park. With its many projections and recessions, its intricately broken roof line, its colorful wall-tile patterns, and its great profusion of blossoming and trailing plants, the exterior of the house was rich to the point of sumptuousness—and yet surprisingly unpretentious, by reason of its low sprawling form and by virtue of the fact that one cannot see more than a small part of the total structure from any one point of view.

On studying the plan, one discovers that the whole scheme is governed by a rectilinear module, corresponding in size to the window-mullion interval, and by major and minor axes which are explicitly marked out on the plan Wright published in 1908; but while the rectilinear system lends a certain stateliness to the design, it is on the whole unobtrusive. Certainly it is not felt to be related, in this case, to the gridiron plan of the city; the streets of Riverside are winding and irregular and provide no basis for our seeing the Coonley house as part of a larger urban composition.

Manson gives us an excellent description of the interior:

> It is a fascinating experience to walk up one of the twin staircases from the entrance lobby into the great living space with its spatial surprises and its fantasy of moving, sloping ceilings emphasizing the fact that we are now under the great hovering roof itself. Here and there are leaded skylights set in separate peaked ceilings where the roofs have broken their flow to adjust themselves to the narrowed spots in plan caused by the joining of one element to another. In all this geometry of space and form, nature is con-

stantly glimpsed through batteries of open casements in the distance, and is introduced into the room by jars of bittersweet and living plants. Across the long north wall, interrupted only by the raked brickwork of the enormous fireplace, there is a dim, painted frieze of a birch forest. These main spaces of the Coonley house combine to make what one is tempted to call a "noble apartment," for they have an undeniable grandeur, with their long vistas and their air of moneyed ease. Yet, the term conjures up the vision of monumental height, and there is no height here; on the contrary, everything is consciously scaled down to man. Wright replaces a sense of lavishness of height with a complete freedom of lateral movement, a luxury that human beings can *use*.[7]

That this extravagant horizontal spaciousness is appreciably more *useful* than the extravagant vertical spaciousness of the Middle Ages seems doubtful, especially in view of the small size of the Coonley family. I would argue, rather, that this broken, rambling horizontal extension seemed to Wright to connote as fitly the meaning of personal freedom in the individual's "social space" as had the loftiness of the cathedral the meaning of order and authority. The one is related to man's ability to turn in many directions, to stroll about and recline at ease, the other, to his having to face in a single direction and to stand "at attention" within a highly regulated social situation. In both cases it is the architectural metaphor that is paramount, apart from considerations of utility.

> I sometimes dream [wrote Thoreau] of a larger and more populous house, standing in a golden age, of enduring materials, and without gingerbread work, which shall still consist of only one room, a vast, rude, substantial, primitive hall, without ceiling or plastering, with bare rafters and purlins . . . wherein you must reach up a torch upon a pole to see the roof, . . . where to be a guest is to be presented with the freedom of the house, and not to be carefully excluded from seven eighths of it, shut up in a particular cell and told to make yourself at home there,—in solitary confinement.[8]

Although the Coonley house is anything but rude or primitive or one-roomed, the spaciousness of its great living room relates more to Thoreau's dream of the free man's abode than to the practical necessities of domestic life. And yet its "air of moneyed ease" would surely have filled Thoreau with dismay. . . .

7. *Ibid.*, pp. 191-93.
8. Thoreau, *Walden* (1854), Chapter 13.

Wright describes the Coonley residence as "the most successful of my houses from my standpoint." [9] An illuminating phrase, that—"from my standpoint." Whether or not the house proved satisfactory to the Coonleys we do not know; but then perhaps it was not built for them at all. It was a splendid image, created by its architect to declare his intuitive understanding of what it means for a free man to possess a social space in a spacious and beneficent world; it is the house one feels Wright would have built for himself at that time if he could have afforded to do so—a "populous" house that seems to cry aloud for the presence of a large and noisy family such as his own. (Mr. Coonley was almost exactly the same age as Wright, so it must have been easy for the latter to identify himself with his client.) By contrast, his crowded little house in Oak Park must have seemed insufferably cramped and confining.

Mr. Coonley's affluence was as a drop in the bucket, however, by comparison with that of Wright's other "palace" patron. Harold Fowler McCormick, vice president of the International Harvester Corporation and husband of John D. Rockefeller's daughter, was the principal heir to one of America's gigantic fortunes. He, too, was attracted by Wright's work, and in 1907 he "proposed that [Wright] should present some ideas in sketch form for a new McCormick family seat in Lake Forest, some thirty miles north of Chicago. The site for this project was a large tract of land bordering the bluffs which rise from the beaches of Lake Michigan." [10] This is as extensive a description of the transaction as has ever been published; I presume that Manson learned from Wright everything the latter could recall or wanted to recall about this ill-fated undertaking.

PLATE XIX

What was called for was not simply a house for Mr. and Mrs. McCormick but a "family seat"—a building that would serve as a family gathering place and as an adequate symbol of the McCormicks' dominant position in the Chicago world. To fulfill these requirements Wright turned to another kind of symbolism and devised a house that would seem rooted in the landscape itself. Toward the lake it was to have raised a façade some three hundred feet wide, rising steeply in

9. *Autobiography,* p. 161.
10. Manson, *Frank Lloyd Wright to 1910,* p. 201.

three tiers above the precipitous bluffs; while on the opposite side it was to have trailed outward for a hundred and thirty feet or more in three low, rambling extensions that conformed to the rolling shape of the land.

A great deal has been written over the years concerning the adjustment of Wright's houses to their natural sites; yet the fact has not been sufficiently appreciated that one sees virtually nothing of this in his work prior to 1902. It could scarcely have been otherwise, for his early residences were erected on relatively small, flat lots on the straight, level streets of Chicago's suburbs. His preoccupation with a correlative relationship between building and site emerges in 1902, and in connection with structures that were outside the city. Perhaps the earliest expression of this concern is to be found in the Hillside Home School buildings of that year. To the same year belong the summer cottages of the Gerts family at Birch Brook, Michigan, and the Charles S. Ross summer cottage at Lake Delavan, Wisconsin. The first really striking exploitation of the site, however, is achieved in the Glasner cottage at Glencoe, Illinois (1905). The little dwelling was originally to have had a separate tea house across a bridged ravine, but this was never built. Because of the tiny scale and truncated nature of the executed building, little of what Wright had in mind comes through in a photograph. It is rather in the presentational drawing for the house that we find grounds for believing that the architect had now gained an altogether new insight into the possibility of interweaving landscape and architecture.

PLATE XX

The principle of reciprocity with site stands against the principle by means of which Wright represents urban or communal order. As we have already observed, even the freest of his city houses yet preserves much of the geometrical formality of the straight street and the rectangular block. That the matter is not simply an aesthetic but rather a metaphorical one is demonstrated, it would seem, by the fact that on the rugged site of Como Orchards the architect was prepared to incur the considerable expense of raising many of the fifty-three box-like houses on high basement podia in order to preserve a common roof line between and among those that were to be seen as members of a group: the irregularities of the site were positively an impediment to the proper expression of communality. The Glasner house, by contrast, was a *private* house, set apart from the regularities of the built-up suburb.

Perhaps it seemed to Wright when he received Mr. McCormick's commission that here at last he would have an opportunity to give full expression to the idea that had been growing in his mind and that was so poorly realized in the Glasner house as it stood. But there were difficulties. Mrs. McCormick was opposed to the project from the beginning and refused even to look at his drawings. What she wanted and eventually got was an imposing Italian villa. Although her conduct in this matter, as in others, was not altogether rational, she may have had her reasons; the McCormicks' position in the Chicago world was unquestionably more Medicean than Thoreauistic. Possibly her adamancy moved Wright to compromise; possibly he himself felt that a family seat for the McCormicks could be no rustic cottage but had to reflect in some way the power and prestige of its owners. At any rate, the block-wide façade above the lake-shore bluffs was to have been perfectly symmetrical, governed by the kind of axiality the architect was later to disparage in domestic design. Even when he was given a spacious site away from the city, the nature of his rich new clients was such that he had to introduce a considerable measure of institutional formality.

The Failure of Success

And now to return to the closed road. We have already taken note of the fact that it was not closed by Wright's failure to win popular approval. By 1909 many of the ideas he had advanced, often in the face of opposition, had been accepted throughout the country. The Victorian ostentatiousness of the 1880s was extinct. Simple, straight-forward ways of building in brick, stone, and plain wood were as popular as Mission furniture and the shirtwaist dress. So far as domestic architecture was concerned, even the *bête noire* of eclecticism was in retreat.

Yet it was just this popular success that must have brought home to Wright the fact that his problem was not to be solved simply by lining the streets of every American suburb with houses in the new style, even if he were to design them all himself. For the plain fact was that the more widely the new manner came to be accepted, the more narrowly he found himself imprisoned within the confines of a fashionable convention. When he had moved to Oak Park in 1890, the streets had been still unpaved and the few houses that were dotted about the undeveloped terrain were of cluttered and ornate design. The situation was an open one in which it seemed a young crusader could surely strike a blow for a freer, simpler, better way of life. Wright's first client, Mr. Winslow, had had to duck down the back streets of River Forest on his way to the station in order to avoid the banter of his fellow commuters, who thought his new-fangled house rather comical. Fifteen years later, however, there was little question of making a resolute stand against empty pretentiousness. By that time a Heurtley or a Willets house would have been considered acceptable in almost any American neighborhood. Oak Park had come to be filled with houses which, even though they were of indifferent quality, nevertheless had more in common with Wright's work than with the old Scovill residence that had represented entrenched iniquity to Mr. Sullivan's young prodigy. Once this change of taste had come about (and certainly Wright could not claim that he had brought it about single-handedly), there came the third- and fourth-rate imitations and adaptations, of which there are many in and around Oak Park—drab, plain houses erected by local builders in a rectilinear, unornamented manner that must have commended itself to them chiefly for reasons of economy.

While all this no doubt contributed to Wright's disenchantment, its principal source would seem rather to have lain, as I have already suggested, in his dawning recognition of the fact that he had not accomplished what he had set out to do. He had intended to win for the free, outspoken, Whitmanesque individual a new kind of membership in the urban community—one that would simultaneously make for greater personal freedom and for greater collective solidarity. Gradually he must have come to realize that what he wanted was at once to reshape the city into a closely knit "family of families" and also to declare that the free man who is true to himself can have no place in the city at all but must make his home in the openness of the natural landscape. Oak Park was at best a poor compromise, at worst the embodiment of a new conventionality, less extravagant but no less stereotyped than that of the 1880s.

Furthermore, we can see why the chief symbol of his dilemma should have lain in his relationship to his own family, for it was in his role as husband and as father of six children that he knew himself to be inextricably involved in the tepid complacency of suburban society. Perhaps there is more truth than their author realized in John Lloyd Wright's remarks about his father's relationship to his fellow citizens:

> They thought him an eccentric visionary because his ideals and even the house that was our home were different from theirs. Her clients were subjected to ridicule—a "crazy" architect built "freak houses" for them. He didn't think, act or dress like the fathers of the day, but was married like them and this, only, gave him the right to be at liberty.[11]

No matter what else he might do or say, the normality of his marriage reassured everyone as to his rightmindedness.

Whitman and Thoreau had been bachelors. So had Courbet, whose conception of self so resembled Wright's own. (Can one imagine M. Bruyas's saying, "Bonjour, M. et Mme. Courbet et vos six enfants"?) Although Emerson was twice married and had children, he had renounced his chosen profession of preaching because of its doctrinal and institutional limitations, and had lived an independent life as essayist and lecturer. "Society everywhere," he had written, "is in conspiracy against the manhood of its members. . . . Whoso would be a man, must be a nonconformist." This had been the message of Wright's *Work Song* in 1896—but by 1909 his work had not only become popular, it had begun to attract the approving attention of such mainstays of the Establishment as Henry Ford and Harold McCormick, whose patronage held out not the promise of success, as Manson thinks, but the threat of destruction. It was Wright's very success that was destroying his self-image, for how could he compare himself with Whitman and Thoreau while putting his art in the service of such multimillionaires?

His marriage had been launched, in the face of parental opposition, as a youthful assertion of freedom and independence; but as Nietzsche had pointed out two years before that marriage took place, "Liberal institutions straightway cease from being liberal the moment they are soundly established: Once this is attained no more grievous

11. John Lloyd Wright, *My Father Who Is on Earth,* p. 25.

and more thorough enemies of freedom exist than liberal institutions." [12] Wright was being forced at last to confront the fact that architecture is the art of established institutions, and that there lay in the very fact of their establishment something that was inherently inimical to his Emersonian ideals. Somewhere he had miscalculated; and so now he found himself facing a "dead wall."

He could not go on. If his work were to have meaning again he would have to make a new beginning. But how and where and on what basis? At the time he could not say. "Because I did not know what I wanted I wanted to go away." In some inarticulate way he knew he wanted freedom—not freedom to do something, for new opportunities were coming to him every day in architecture, but freedom to be a different man from the one he was being made into. It is not surprising that Mrs. Wright, on whom the burden of rearing a large family on an inadequate and often squandered income had no doubt fallen heavily, should have neither understood that necessity nor sympathized with her husband's feeling that he was being defeated by his success. She had no reason to feel that their life in Oak Park had proved a failure, and probably he could not have explained why he somehow felt it had. A barrier arose between them, the source and nature of which neither of them, apparently, could identify.

During the second half of the year 1909 there gradually evolved in Wright's mind a course of action (one can hardly call it a plan) which would permit him to escape from his difficulties, even though it might not resolve them. Toward the end of October he quickly raised what money he could and left Chicago for New York, where, by prearrangement, he met Mrs. Cheney and sailed with her for Europe. What the immediate and conscious motivations of the two of them may have been it is impossible to say. Manson sees Wright "exactly duplicating his father's behaviour in 1885" and suggests that the architect had inherited something of his father's emotional instability and stubborn wilfulness. Possibly he had, but the conditions of his departure were as different as they could well be from those attending his father's: whereas William Cary Wright had been rejected by his strong-willed wife and had sought divorce in order to free himself from an intoler-

12. Nietzsche, *The Twilight of the Idols* (1888), Part 10.

able domestic situation, his son Frank was so dearly loved by his wife Catherine that she refused for thirteen years to believe that he would not eventually come back to her, in order to resume a family life that had for the most part been, it would seem, extraordinarily happy. "He was an epic of wit and merriment," his son John recalls, "that gave our home the feeling of a jolly carnival." Two occasions could hardly have been more unlike.

John Lloyd Wright leaves us with the impression that it was all a matter of his father's having "fallen in love" again. No doubt he had; but for a man in Wright's position—having a wife and six children, a flourishing practice in domestic architecture, and an oft-avowed concern for all that pertains to the virtues and integrity of the life of the family—deliberately to pursue a course over an extended period of time that would inevitably result in scandal and in the destruction of that position must surely reveal deeper and more compelling motivations than are ordinarily suggested by the phrase "falling in love." What they were no one will ever fully know. All the evidence we have would seem to indicate that they had as much to do with his architectural practice as with his no doubt genuine affection for Mamah Cheney.

For on the day of his departure he took the odd and quite unnecessary step of turning that practice over to a man he hardly knew—one Herman von Holst, a German-born architect who had no particular knowledge of or sympathy for Wright's work. He could have left it in the hands of his own capable staff; it was they who had to carry out the work of the Studio in any case. But by leaving without so much as a word to either his wife or his helpers, he repudiated both his home and his work. Had he wanted simply a respite during which to reassess his position, he could have gone to Berlin by himself; but by going with Mrs. Cheney he deliberately flouted the very conventions that are ordinarily upheld and defended by domestic architecture. It must have seemed to Wright that in defying law and custom he was breaking his way out of the trap of conventionality in which he felt himself to be caught—yet even then his feelings were deeply equivocal and ambivalent, for after spending a year in Europe with Mrs. Cheney, he returned home to his family in the fall of 1910 and remained with them, off and on, until the end of the following year . . . though on just what terms we do not know. That there was something inherently good in Victorian domesticity Wright could not categorically deny, any more than he could affirm that that goodness was satisfying and sufficient.

FIVE

A NEW BEGINNING AND ITS DESTRUCTION

WHEN WRIGHT LEFT CHICAGO IN 1909 HE plainly had not thought the matter through to the point of deciding how and where he and Mrs. Cheney would live, or even of foreseeing that because of their "private" action they would be mercilessly pilloried in the press and vilified by public opinion. Nor did he formulate any specific plans for the future, so far as we can tell, during the many months they lived abroad, mainly in Berlin and in Fiesole. His was a difficult predicament, for it is in the nature of the architect's function that he cannot, as can the painter and the poet, practice his art as a Bohemian or an outcast. He must be acceptable to at least some segment of the reputable and established community. In asserting his freedom to live an unconventional life Wright had jeopardized his acceptability, especially as a domestic architect. What he had to do now was to make clear, both to himself and to the public, the ethical basis of his new orientation. So far as his relation to his family and to Mrs. Cheney was concerned, he had reached certain conclusions about love and law which seemed to him to justify his actions.[1] How they bore upon architecture, however, was another matter. At the time he could not say.

The Dimensions of the Problem

As late as the spring of 1914, when he published his second article "In the Cause of Architecture," he was still unable to do so. The essay is an unrelievedly morose diatribe against the stultification and corruption that had beset the "new school" because of the machinations of imitators, popularizers, exploiters, brokers, counterfeiters, neophytes, "disciples," quacks, advertizers, traders, seducers, hypocrites, language-speakers, parasites, ego-maniacs, and so on. His only positive assertions are that the style of every architect must grow out of his direct grappling with materials and out of his own individuality—even as had his own style when he had entered the field twenty-one years before, "alone, absolutely alone"—and that no man should draw in-

1. These conclusions are summarized in his *Autobiography* on pp. 163-64. They were probably influenced, as Edgar Kaufmann has observed, by Ellen K. S. Key's tract on free love, which he had helped to translate and publish in 1912.

spiration from the forms of another man's work—though of course all proper styles must be based upon the same natural and organic principle. Despite his own recent and continuing difficulties with the institutions of family and city, he does not suggest that the development of a new style might require a re-examination of those institutional structures and of their relation to the free individual. Instead, he finds the basis of style to lie in the interaction of materials and personality.

Yet there are a few lines in which a glimmering of new insight appears. Gone is his earlier enthusiasm for the democratic vista.

> The "Democracy" of the man in the American street is no more than the Gospel of Mediocrity. When it is understood that a great Democracy is the highest form of Aristocracy conceivable, not of birth or place or wealth, but of those qualities that give distinction to the man as man, and that as a social state it must be characterized by the honesty and responsibility of the absolute individualist as the unit of its structure, then only can we have an Art worthy of the name.[2]

Here at last the crux of the difficulty is plainly stated: it lies in Wright's conception of a society composed of wholly responsible yet absolutely free individualists—a society in which "we" (in the plural) shall produce "an Art" (in the singular) that will be worthy of taking its place among the great styles in which Wright had steeped himself during his sojourn in Europe. The problem is as old as the hills—that of reconciling freedom with responsibility. Whoever responds "responsibly" to the needs and purposes of his fellow citizens will perforce have his individuality modified and conditioned by theirs. Inevitably it had been the judgment of society that in proving himself an "absolute" individualist by abandoning his sizable family, Wright had been grossly irresponsible. He insisted that his right to complete freedom justified that course of action. Although he later acknowledged that he had suffered acute anguish after leaving his wife and children, he never admitted that his departure might have caused them as great or greater anguish for which he might have been held responsible.

These were the ethical problems with which he had to wrestle. When he had written his 1908 article, he had seemed scarcely aware

2. "In the Cause of Architecture," *Architectural Record,* XXXV: 5 (May 1914), 412.

of their existence. By 1914 he was just beginning to achieve a clear understanding of the implications of the Rousseauistic view of man to which he had always clung. "He who would preserve the supremacy of natural feelings in social life," wrote Rousseau, "knows not what he asks. Ever at war with himself, hesitating between his wishes and his duties, he will be neither a man nor a citizen." [3] By decamping with his neighbor's wife, Wright had perhaps proved his manly freedom; it remained for him now, as an architect, to demonstrate its relationship to the city and to citizenship. For architecture pertains to *res publica;* it is not simply a matter of self-expression.

Plato argues that goodness or justice is what makes it possible for men to combine[4]—from which it follows for him that regularity, right proportion, and conformity to ideal standards are virtuous, that eccentricity and excess are reprehensible, and that an absolute individualist, if there could be such a thing, would be absolutely evil. This is the conception of goodness that the Parthenon proclaims to the city of Athens, and this has been the message of the classic orders ever since. Louis Sullivan dismissed the idea as "feudal," and from him his pupil learned contempt for "this pseudo-search of the Greeks for the elegant imposition." [5] Nevertheless, in those aspects of his architecture that had borne upon public and collective experience Wright had relied, as we have seen, upon patterns in which regularity and conformity were of the greatest importance. By his own actions he had now rejected the validity of those standardizing patterns. Could there be found, then, another basis of order, one that would sustain social and collective relationships, but that would not require the patterned conformity that he had formerly associated with the city but had now disavowed? By 1914 he had not found it, but he was coming to understand the dimensions of the problem.

3. Jean-Jacques Rousseau, *Emile,* trans. Barbara Foxley (London: J. M. Dent & Sons, Ltd., 1911), p. 8.

4. "For we have already shown that the just are wiser and better and abler than the unjust, and that the unjust are incapable of common action; nay more, than to speak as we did of men who are evil acting vigorously together, is not strictly true, for if they had been perfectly evil, they would have laid hands upon one another; but it is evident that there must have been some remnant of justice in them, which enabled them to combine." *Republic I, 352* (Jowett translation).

5. *Genius and Mobocracy,* p. 84.

PERHAPS THE decision that had the greatest influence on the shaping of a new departure was made not by Wright himself but by his mother. The elder Mrs. Wright had followed her son to Chicago in the 1880s and had lived nearby during his years in Oak Park. Perceiving, it appears, that he had irremediably alienated himself from the respectable community of suburban Chicago, she took steps to acquire for him, while he was still in Europe, a low hill in the valley of the Lloyd-Joneses near Spring Green; and it was there, in the summer of 1911, that Wright began to build for himself and Mrs. Borthwick (Mr. Cheney had sued for divorce on the grounds of desertion, and she had resumed her maiden name) a new kind of home, unlike any he had built in Oak Park—though it was to bear some relationship to his earlier country cottages and to the McCormick project.

So it was, then, that Wright established himself in the country rather than in the city after his return from "voluntary exile." "Yes, a retreat when I returned from Europe in 1911. I began to build Taliesin to get my back against the wall and fight for what I saw I had to fight." [6] In 1914 he could not say just what that was; he does not mention the novelty of Taliesin in his second article. But some sixteen years later he could say clearly what it had all meant to him:

PLATE XXI

> I turned to this hill in the Valley as my Grandfather before me had turned to America—as a hope and haven. . . . And architecture by now was quite mine. It had come to me by actual experience and meant something out of this ground we call America. Architecture was something in league with the stone of the field, in sympathy with "the flower that fadeth and the grass that withereth." It had something of the prayerful consideration for the lilies of the field that was my gentle grandmother's: something natural to the great change that was America herself.
>
> It was unthinkable to me, at least unbearable, that any house should be put *on* that beloved hill.
>
> I knew well that no house should ever be *on* a hill or *on* anything. It should be *of* the hill. Belonging to it. Hill and house should live together each the happier for the other. That was the way everything found round about was naturally managed except when man did something. When he added his mite he became imitative and ugly. Why? Was there

6. *Autobiography*, p. 167.

no natural house? I felt I had proved there was. Now I wanted a natural house to live in myself. I scanned the hills of the region where the rock came cropping out in strata to suggest buildings. How quiet and strong the rock-ledge masses looked with the dark red cedars and white birches, there, above the green slopes. They were all part of the countenance of southern Wisconsin.

I wished to be part of my beloved southern Wisconsin, too. I did not want to put my small part of it out of countenance. Architecture, after all, I have learned—or before all, I should say—is no less a weaving and a fabric than the trees are. . . .

There must be a natural house, not natural as caves and log-cabins were natural, but native in spirit and the making, having itself all that architecture had meant whenever it was alive in times past. Nothing at all I had ever seen would do. This country had changed all that old building into something inappropriate. Grandfather and Grandmother were something splendid in themselves that I couldn't imagine living in any of the period-houses I had ever seen or the ugly ones around there. Yes, there was a house that hill might marry and live happily with ever after. I fully intended to find it. I even saw for myself what it might be like. And I began to build it as the brow of that hill. . . .

The slabs of great stone went down for pavements of terraces and courts. Stone was sent along the slopes into great walls. Stone stepped up like ledges on to the hill and flung long arms in any direction that brought the house to the ground. The ground! My Grandfather's ground. It was lovingly felt as intimate in all this.

Finally it was not so easy to tell where pavements and walls left off and ground began. Especially on the hill-crown, which became a low-walled garden above the surrounding courts, reached by stone steps walled into the slopes. A clump of fine oaks that grew on the hilltop stood untouched on one side above the court. A great curved stone-walled seat enclosed the space just beneath them and stone pavement stepped down to a spring or fountain that welled up into a pool at the center of the circle. . . .

A house of the North. The whole was low, wide and snug, a broad shelter seeking fellowship with its surroundings. A house that could open to the breezes of summer and become like an open camp if need be. With spring came music on the roofs, for there were few dead roof-spaces overhead, and the broad eaves so sheltered the windows that they were safely left open to the sweeping soft air of the rain. . . .

It was intensely human, I believe.[7]

7. *Ibid.*, pp. 168-74.

Why could not Wright have written thus "in the cause of architecture" in 1914, instead of producing the dour lament he saw fit to publish when the first Taliesin was at the peak of its beauty? These paragraphs alone would have been worth more than all fourteen of his later "In the Cause" essays. Perhaps it is the distinguishing gift of the genuine artist that he thinks directly in terms of shapes and expresses himself verbally only afterward, if ever at all. Taliesin was a rich and subtle embodiment of an idea of which Wright had achieved at best only a partial and inadequate expression heretofore—the idea of a spacious, rambling symbol of the family, rooted not in the arbitrary grid of the city but in Nature itself. Visually the idea was worked out between 1911 and 1914, but there is little to indicate that a verbalization of these insights had even begun to take shape at that time. Wright was not prepared to repudiate what he had done in Oak Park, for such fame as he had depended upon that achievement. Not being able to say what had gone awry in the development of the new architecture he had envisioned, he could only direct a censorious broadside against the entire business of building, buying, and selling houses in a middle-class suburban society.

How long it would have taken in the normal course of events for the new standpoint to find verbal statement we cannot say. Possibly its advancement as a general principle would have had to wait upon further development of the automobile and the highway, which were to make widely available the kind of remote country residence we are familiar with today and of which the first Taliesin was a precursor. Be that as it may, in August 1914, there occurred two disasters which postponed for many years a fulfilment of the promise that was contained in the new house Wright had built.

Years of Uprootedness

OF THE greatest immediate importance, of course, was the frightful destruction of Taliesin on August 15th. At lunchtime on that day a paranoid servant, one Julian Carlston, went berserk, set fire to the house, and killed seven persons, including Mrs. Borthwick and her two children, who happened to be visiting her at the time. Wright was in Chicago, winding up work on the Midway Gardens. He reached Spring

Green after dark that night, to find that the new and unconventional life in which he had found such happiness, and of which the house itself was the purest expression, had been annihilated.

In order to fill the terrible emptiness that possessed him after the holocaust he set to work at once to raise a new and better Taliesin, but he could not by himself make it a meaningful home. There follows, then, a period of some twelve years or more when he was seldom at Spring Green. His time was spent mainly in Japan and in California and Arizona, though these were years when he was continually moving from place to place. It was an interlude of rootlessness and of restless experimentation with the technics of building that produced little or nothing that was relevant to the vein of architectural imagery that had been, and would later continue to be, the very stuff of his art.

Yet I believe we cannot understand the architect's seeming impotence in the 1920s without taking fully into account the other disaster of 1914—the outbreak of war, which had preceded the destruction at Taliesin by thirteen days. Its effect was not immediately felt in this country, but eventually the involvement of the United States brought with it a vehemently emotional outburst of nationalistic and anti-German feeling in which Wright, who was out of the country much of the time, could have had no part. Both his Whitmanesque conception of American democracy and his abiding love of "Old Germany" stood opposed to all such manifestations. Partly because of his Rousseauistic convictions, partly because of the abusive notoriety he had lately suffered, he felt that he stood outside this "unnaturally excited" situation. He hated conscription and all that it implied in the way of regimentation and violence.

Then, as if this were not a sufficient cause of alienation between him and his countrymen, the war was followed by a quick, fierce reaction against the mores with which we associate the Gibson Girl, Chautauqua, Arts and Crafts, Mission furniture, and the Prairie house. Perhaps nothing better illustrates the abrupt change in the public temper than the fate of Wright's Midway Gardens—a project that was conceived just before the war to suit the tastes of that day (in which effort it was superbly successful) and which, by the end of the war, had become a useless irrelevancy, already shabbily cheapened and soon to be demolished. The idea has gained currency in some circles that what ruined the Gardens was Prohibition, but Wright makes it plain that this was not at all the case: the Gardens' first season—that of 1914—was its only really successful one. After a shaky and badly managed second season it was sold to a brewing company and converted into a plebeian beer garden that its architect found unbearably offensive. It was because "the course of normal life everywhere was soon upset" by the emotional impact of the war that Wright's architectural fantasy, seeming "strange to all" and awakening "a sense of mystery and romance in the beholder," ceased to attract customers and fell by the wayside.

I find that elderly persons who have read about Wright in the newspapers from time to time over the years still think of him as having been a rake, libertine, or worse. (An aging architect recently assured me that he knew for a fact that Wright had had seven wives.) But to see in his "spiritual hegira," as the reporters called it, an anticipation of the moral revolt of the twenties would be to mistake it completely. In his own eyes, at least, his flight had been motivated by the highest ethical principles and the purest ideal of love. The spirit in which he turned to Taliesin in 1911 was the one we find expressed in Courbet's "Lovers in the Country" and in the verses with which the book *House Beautiful* concludes:

> I dreamed of Paradise,—and still,
> Though sun lay soft on vale and hill,
> And trees were green and rivers bright,
> The one dear thing that made delight
> By sun or stars or eden weather,
> Was just that we two were together.

But this was the kind of sentiment (or sentimentality, as it would have been called) that was skeptically "debunked" in the post-war decade. To those who set the pace of popular American life in that jazzy age of flappers and speakeasies, and who were enjoying to the fullest its unparalleled commercial prosperity, the ideals of Emerson and Thoreau must have seemed hopelessly *passé*—perhaps seemed so even to Wright himself. He was living not only in an age that would not listen, but in one to which he had nothing to say. In the thirteen short articles "In the Cause of Architecture" that were published in the *Record* in 1927-1928, we find little that is fresh or cogent.

We have seen that between 1900 and 1910 Wright was much interested in blocks—both city blocks and block-like architectural compositions of various sorts. In the 1920s he entered a "block period" of altogether another kind. He became fascinated with designing complicated little blocks and with "weaving" little ones together into larger blocks. At a time when he was not only adrift but was being hounded and harassed as few men in our country have ever been, the purely constructive processes of shaping and fitting seemed enormously appealing to him and even appeared to hold the promise of an all-inclusive architectural reformation.

Other buildings sprang full-born into my mind from this humble beginning. They arose in bewildering variety and peerless beauty. Gradually all complications, all needless expense of the treacherous and wasteful building system of a whole country, all went by the board. Any humble cottage might now live as architecture with integrity known only in former ages. At last, here I was grasping the near-end of a great means to a finer order." [8]

No longer was he concerned with family and city. The road to architectural salvation seemed to lie for him, as it did for so many others in the wake of World War I, in the development of new ways of putting together a building—any building, regardless of its size or purpose. His articles "In the Cause of Architecture" from the 1920s deal almost exclusively with the properties of materials and with design procedures, with an arid and abstract constructivism that has no bearing upon his earlier purposes and concerns.

The handful of structures that were built at the time look like "blockhouses" in more senses of the word than one. In fact, even before the first of the textile-block residences was undertaken Wright had revealed in his design for the Barnsdall house a taste for impenetrable massiveness and austerity that is quite foreign to his earlier work. We can understand all this in terms of the personal anxieties of the architect, but it is hard to find here an affirmation concerning *res publica* or the image of the family that can be compared to what we see in both earlier and later buildings. He was working in a world to which he

PLATE XXII

8. *Ibid.*, p. 246.

felt he did not belong, a world where he had no roots and no place, and where his chief need was not to define the nature of his participation but simply to be sheltered and made secure.

Speaking of Aline Barnsdall, Wright says,

> My client, I soon found, had ideas and wanted yours but never worked much nor for long at a time, being possessed by incorrigible wanderlust that made me wonder, sometimes, what she wanted a beautiful home for—anyhow, anywhere. Later, I came to see that *that* was just *why* she wanted one.[9]

This was another house the architect might well have described as being especially satisfactory *from his standpoint*; as with Mr. and Mrs. Coonley, he had found in Miss Barnsdall a client with whom he could readily identify himself, for he was in much the same situation as she. The house was important to him; he devotes ten pages of his *Autobiography* to it.

> I would hear from her when I was wandering about in the maze of the Imperial Hotel in Japan while she was in Hollywood. She would get my telegrams or letters in Spain when I eventually got to Hollywood. And I would hear from her in New York while I was in Chicago or San Francisco. Or, hear from her from some remote piney mountain retreat in the Rockies when I was sea-sick out on the Pacific Ocean.[10]

His circumstances could scarcely have been more different from those he had known in Oak Park or was later to know at Taliesin; little wonder that the houses of this trying period are different in form and meaning from all his other works.

An illuminating episode from the mid-twenties, at a time when his nation looked upon him as a pariah, was Wright's gratuitous effort at designing for the city of New York (a city that had seemed indifferent to his existence) a "Steel Cathedral embracing minor cathedrals"—a mammoth tent-like structure of steel and glass, as tall as the Empire State Building was later to be and large enough to hold a million worshipers. Its size, in relationship to that of the city as a whole, would have made its position comparable to that of the great cathedrals in the little French cities of the thirteenth century. Hitchcock describes the

9. *Ibid.*, p. 227.
10. *Idem.*

project, or dismisses it, as being "really fantastic and economically unrealizable." [11] Obviously the building was totally unrelated to any economic or institutional situation, in New York or anywhere else, so that to criticize its practicality is irrelevant. Yet the project seems full of meaning and pathos because it reveals so intense a preoccupation with membership and agreement on the part of a man who knew himself to be a rootless outcast. Wright would have liked to be a cathedral builder, the acknowledged spokesman for the ideal unity of his city. But the city was not his own, it knew nothing of a unifying faith, and it could not have cared less about him or his ideals.

The Steel Cathedral attests to Wright's continuing bafflement and helplessness before the problem of the city. Eighteen years after his flight from Chicago he was still utterly unable to address the American city with forms that could be said to have a significant bearing upon either the life of the community or the constitution of the state; and because he could not do so, even the houses he was building lack the cogency that the best works from his Oak Park years so plainly possessed. As was observed at the outset, architecture is an art of urban man; it is to him that it speaks in even its most anti-urban manifestations.

11. Henry-Russell Hitchcock, *In the Nature of Materials* (New York: Duell, Sloane, and Pearce, 1942), p. 82.

SIX
DEPRESSION AND RESURGENCE

BY THE YEAR 1931, WRITES HITCHCOCK, "IT WAS easy . . . to see Wright chiefly as an old master, his life's work done, filling out his years by lecturing and writing his reminiscences; inveighing at the audacities of the young and bemusing himself and the world with occasional projects of an apparently quite fantastic character."[1] Although the country had just experienced a building boom of unprecedented proportions, Wright had built almost nothing. However, just as a concatenation of private and public events had in 1914 deflected him from what appeared to be a promising course of development, so, too, was he set on course again by another such concurrence some fifteen years later. First, there was the entrance into his life of Olgivanna (Olga Ivanovna Milanoff) and the rebuilding of Taliesin after the fire of 1925. The wretched Miriam Noel affair was not immediately brought to an end, but by 1928, after a final episode of persecution at the hands of the law and the press, he was safely married again and at work on lucrative projects. Once again he had a family and a place that was his and theirs in the valley where his family had had a secure place since before he was born.

Anti-Urbanism and the Revival of the Family

Yet his engrossment with blocks persisted, giving rise to the Chandler projects of 1927-28 and the Richard Lloyd-Jones house of 1929 (the latter a strangely dry and mechanistic building, perhaps the least attractive house—the least *domestic*—that Wright ever built). The public event that completed his reorientation was, I believe, the Great Depression of the early thirties. Wright was always at heart something of a preacher, missionary, and reformer; but amidst the booming and roaring of the twenties he had been hard put to know what to say. By a stroke of good fortune, he had been able, not long after the disaster at Taliesin in 1914, to immerse himself completely in the demanding task of erecting the Imperial Hotel. That project removed him for awhile from the social context in which his earlier work had been done and in which he had later suffered notoriety and persecution, and it

1. Henry-Russell Hitchcock, "Frank Lloyd Wright at the Museum of Modern Art," *Art Bulletin,* XXIII (March 1941), 73.

provided him with a job that turned more upon an objective problem in engineering than upon metaphorical expression. From that constructivist experience he had gone on to others—a drift that must have been speeded by the spectacular survival of the hotel in the great earthquake of 1923. (In later years Wright never tired of retelling the story of that survival, as if it were a prime authentication of the originality and excellence of modern architecture; whereas in fact the building was peripheral to the main course of his own career and to the development of modern building in general.)

The depression put an abrupt end to projects in this vein. There followed a period of four years when Wright built nothing at all. During this time he surveyed the shape of his career by writing his *Autobiography*, took stock of his position, organized the Taliesin Fellowship, and prepared the way for a new surge of creativity in the middle thirties.

It was an era when the need for some kind of reform was acknowledged by almost everyone. In the midst of breakdown Wright was able to step forth in the role that became him best, that of the prophet who speaks out to his nation.

> Yes, I must and I do believe that this new demand for life as organic—therefore life as itself a noble kind of architecture—architecture is life—must read first lessons afresh in the great book of creation itself. . . . A common integrity of life will then carry these . . . significances as one great integrity to full expression as the great Usonian architecture of Life, the great universal life of our own true democracy. America, there is no need to be afraid! [2]

"Comfort ye, comfort ye my people. . . ." This is the language of prophecy. In the midst of depression Wright embraced again that Biblical, Augustinian, Rousseauistic mode of thought in which he had been nurtured and from which he had somewhat turned aside during the twenties. The *Autobiography* itself is related in tone and content to the *Confessions* of both Augustine and Rousseau, and stands in the Romantic tradition that prompted the writing of voluminous personal journals by so many men and women, both prominent and obscure, in the nineteenth century. His renewed affinity with the French philosopher is revealed most clearly in his altered attitude toward nature—an

2. *Autobiography*, p. 351.

attitude that now involved the idea that there is an inherent opposition between nature and the city. Wright had had much to say about nature in his 1908 article: "Her wealth of suggestion is inexhaustible; her riches are greater than any man's desire." [3] The nature he commends to the architect at that time, however, reveals herself in small biological forms, such as wildflowers, wherein she exemplifies the fitness and simplicity that organic architecture should possess. Not until about 1931, when he looked back upon and reassessed his experiences between 1909 and 1914, did there emerge in his writings the idea of a spacious and extensive nature that affords the only suitable habitat for the natural man.

> The modern idea [he could now write] is to seek the spaciousness, openness, lightness, and strength that is now logical and that will scatter urbanism (the city) into the regional field. . . . Every man will soon have facility to roam the sky or ground and live with the perfect freedom of vision that will relate him to the ground and all that the ground should mean to the human life of which he is the whole as he is a part.[4]

To many people the villain of the depression story seemed to be the city of New York. Possibly the strain of anti-urbanism that enters Wright's thinking at this time was shaped in part by this common feeling. Yet it was never in terms of the popular image of "Wall Street" that he conceived the sinister influence of that city, but rather in terms of what seemed to him the false sense of values that lay behind the unnatural ways in which people lived and worked and found entertainment there—ways associated in his mind with the "Cashandcarry mentality" and the "Broadway Creed" of cynical belittlement. He was especially dismayed by the urban individual's loss of independence and self-reliance.

> Men are not made to be crowded together in ant-hills [declared Rousseau] but scattered over the earth to till it. The more they are massed together, the more corrupt they become. . . . Of all creatures man is least fitted to live in herds. . . . Men are devoured by our towns. In a few generations the race dies out or becomes degenerate; it needs renewal, and it is always renewed

3. "In the Cause of Architecture," 1908, p. 155.
4. Frank Lloyd Wright, "What is the Modern Idea?", *Physical Culture,* June 24, 1934. (Article apparently written in 1932.)

from the country. Send your children to renew themselves, so to speak, send them to regain in the open fields the strength lost in the foul air of our crowded cities.[5]

One of the side-effects of the depression was the awakening of a widespread enthusiasm for the country and for the folkways and traditions of country life. Among American artists the new enthusiasm gave rise to the Regionalist movement with which we associate the names of Wood, Curry, Benton, and the like. Once is tempted to place Wright in this company, for certainly there was a connection between his thought and theirs at the time. But though he and they were conditioned by the same situation and responded to it in somewhat similar ways, Wright was more deeply concerned than they, I believe, with fundamental problems of form, order, and meaning. The typical Regionalist painting seems to us today either emptily journalistic (e.g., Curry's "Baptism in Kansas") or pretentiously contrived (e.g., Benton's "Persephone") or simply trite and unrewarding (e.g., the landscapes of Paul Sample). For all their devotion to the soil, the Regionalists had lost touch with the genuine convictions in which landscape and figure-in-landscape painting had been rooted in the nineteenth century. Within less than twenty-five years their paintings, unlike Wright's houses, have already lost their status as consequential works of art. When we compare any one of them with Fallingwater we are struck immediately with the immense difference in the quality of invention. For Wright the issues and ideas with which the generation of Courbet had grappled were still alive, still capable of provoking the creation of new forms. For the painters they were not.

Another side-effect of the depression was the strengthening of family ties and of sympathy for the notion of family solidarity. Whereas in the 1920s the family had been widely attacked, along with other manifestations of traditional institutionalism, in the early thirties, when many families were forced to pool their limited resources, to move together under a single roof, and to find their recreation within the family circle, the strong family unit seemed again desirable, a refuge against the isolation and helplessness of the unemployed individ-

5. *Emile,* pp. 26 and 14.

ual.[6] Although the economic situation was not at all favorable for the domestic architect, the social and psychological one was very much so—as it had not been during the boom period, when houses were built in enormous numbers by architects who had no serious concern or conviction with regard to the family, as one can easily tell by looking at the houses themselves. (It is interesting to note that, of the handful of houses Wright built in the twenties, the only two he discusses in his *Autobiography*—the Barnsdall and Millard residences—were built for single women rather than for families.) It was in part this revival of familism that made possible Wright's distinctive affirmations in the 1930s.

Because of the changes that were suddenly brought about by the depression, then, Wright was prompted to make a number of new statements concerning man's possession of a place in his world. The range of these ideas is encompassed, I believe, by four undertakings that belong to the period between 1932 and 1936: the founding of the Taliesin Fellowship, the erection of the Kaufmann house and of the Johnson Administration building, and the publication of the Broadacre City proposal. These we must consider one by one.

Taliesin: Built To Music

WHAT MOVED Wright to establish the Fellowship, it would seem, was his need for money and for something to do in the depths of the depression. While it did not prove to be a bonanza (that was not its purpose), it did provide the architect with a few thousand dollars a year with which to meet some of the expenses of maintaining and expanding Taliesin, and it furnished a part-time labor force that contributed substantially toward making the enterprise self-sustaining (one of Wright's most cherished goals).

As an educational venture it was inspired, in all likelihood, by the example of at least two earlier institutions. In some ways it perpetuated the ideals of the Hillside Home School, whose buildings it eventually

6. *Vide: Family Life and National Recovery,* prepared by the Committee of the Family Society of Philadelphia (New York, 1935), and Winona L. Morgan, *The Family Meets the Depression* (Minneapolis: University of Minnesota Press, 1939).

incorporated. Like Hillside, it was at once a home, a farm, and a school, although at no point was its schooling as conventional as Hillside's. More important was the example of Elbert Hubbard's Roycroft School. As a visitor wrote in 1912,

> [The Roycroft School] teaches boys and girls something from books. The pupils are taught to work in the open. They are brought in touch with life in the fields. They groom horses, shear sheep, feed the hogs, milk the cows, plant potatoes, pick currants, do all kinds of farmwork. And they do it joyously. . . . They do the toil that fills the larder of the Roycroft Inn. And they pay Elbert Hubbard for the privilege of doing it. Isn't that lovely? [7]

In his first Taliesin prospectus Wright emphasizes his intention (never fully carried out) to give instruction in just those crafts for which East Aurora was noted: typographical design, printing, molding, woodworking, weaving, and so on.

Beyond East Aurora we can trace Taliesin's ancestry back to the Arts and Crafts movement, to Ruskin's Guild of St. George, to various communitarian societies of the nineteenth century, to Overbeck's Nazarenes, and, in general, to the ever-present tendency of romantic thought to exalt the virtues of a quasi-monastic brotherhood of craftsmen. In a number of ways the purpose and program of Taliesin, as they were set forth in the Prospectus, resembled those of Gropius's Bauhaus, which also owed a great debt, of course, to Arts and Crafts.

> We believe that a rational attempt to integrate Art and Industry should coordinate both with the everyday life we live here in America. Any such rational attempt must be *essential architecture* growing up by way of social, industrial, and economic processes natural to our way of life. . . . Each apprentice will work under the inspiration of direct architectural leadership, toward machine-craft art in this machine age.[8]

How much of this was inspired directly by the Bauhaus we do not know. For our purposes it is more important to understand the differences between the two institutions than to define their common background and aims. Though both were concerned with the integration of art and industry, the emphasis at Dessau was on industry, at Spring

7. William Marion Reedy, *A Little Journey to East Aurora* (East Aurora, N. Y., 1912), p. 33. The charge of exploitation that is hinted at here was sometimes made against Wright's scheme, too.

8. *Autobiography,* pp. 390-91.

Green, on art. The Bauhaus looks like a factory (its architecture descends directly from Gropius's Fagus plant at Alfeld), while Taliesin is a rustic country home. Whereas the Bauhaus aggressively supported the modern urban and industrial economy of the postwar world, Taliesin was essentially opposed to it: "The Big City is no longer a place for more than the exterior applications of some cliché or sterile formula, where life is concerned. Therefore the TALIESIN FELLOWSHIP chooses to live and work in the country." [9]

The significance of that gathering in the country can be fully appreciated only in the light of a literary tradition with which the architect must have been well acquainted. He himself hints of the direction in which we should look when he asserts that "Taliesin, a Druid, was a member of King Arthur's Roundtable." For it is in connection with the Taliesin Fellowship that Wright gave fullest expression to a set of ideas that seems closely bound up with that household favorite of the English-speaking Victorian world, the *Idyls of the King*. In his retelling of the Arthurian legends Tennyson performs the remarkable feat of transposing their ethic from chivalrous into Rousseauistic terms. The driving motivation behind his narratives stems less from the ideals of chivalry and of courtly love than from that fateful tension the poet finds to exist between the values of loyalty and of self-fulfillment, between membership in the Round Table and the quest for the Grail. As Arthur foresees even before the first knight sets out upon the search, that quest must eventually bring about the destruction of the knightly brotherhood.[10]

As we have seen, it had been Wright's practice, almost from the beginning of his career in Oak Park, to train young persons in his draughting room—men and women who came because of their enthusiasm for him and for his architecture and who received a small wage as helpers. In so doing he brought his "apprentices" partially within the circle of his own family and made his home a base from

9. *Ibid.*
10. For the interpretation of the *Idyls of the King* upon which this and the following paragraphs are based, I am especially indebted to Edward D. H. Johnson's *The Alien Vision of Victorian Poetry* (Princeton: Princeton University Press, 1952).

which they could go forth to do service "in the cause of architecture."[11] In the following passage he assesses the results of that practice after some thirty-five years:

> Meantime some of the young men who had begun their architectural careers with me were at work out here [in California in the 1920s]—in the midst of the popular falsification as I have described it in this land of the *realtoresque* taken as substitute for the picturesque. What were they all doing to modify popular meanness and qualify imitative Usonia? There were many such—fifty or sixty—young men working in the United States or Europe or Japan as architects by now. They had come to me from all parts of the world to enter into my work. Not so much as students; I am no teacher. They came more as apprentices, beginning with no pay—except their living at Taliesin—or with small pay if more competent to help. . . .
>
> With the exception of some six or seven I have never had reason to complain of their enthusiasm for their work nor of their loyalty to me. But, of their loyalty to the cause—yes. And after all, were they not taken on, in that cause?
>
> This process of natural selection on their part had its advantages. Some disadvantages. Never going out of my way after the material I really need but always taking those who want to come to me—I do make some sacrifices for sympathetic cooperation, oftentimes not so efficient as it should be. I am fond of the flattery of young people. They indulge me and I indulge them. It is easy for them and for me to do this. But they get the idea that when the master's back is turned, to draw his ideas in his own way, or in theirs, does make those ideas and his way their own. Later on, they must do

11. Wright's use of the word apprentice has led some to believe that the model for the Fellowship is to be found in the medieval guild. The idea is sound enough if it be clearly understood that those guilds were originally religious confraternities rather than regulatory associations of craftsmen. "Medieval guilds were voluntary associations formed for the mutual aid and protection of their members. Among the guildsmen there was a strong spirit of fraternal cooperation or Christian brotherhood, with a mixture of worldly and religious ideals—the support of the body and the salvation of the soul. Early meanings of the root *gild* or *geld* were expiation, penalty, sacrifice or worship, feast or banquet, and contribution or payment; it is difficult to determine which is the earliest meaning, and we are not sure whether the gildsmen were originally those who contributed to a common fund or those who worshipped or feasted together." (Charles Gross, "Guilds," *Encyclopedia Britannica* [1948], X, 964.) In this earliest sense of the word, the Taliesin Fellowship may indeed be regarded as a guild, as may also the legendary Round Table. By no means, however, was the Fellowship concerned with the systematic training of journeymen, with the establishment and maintenance of standards, or with any of the restrictive functions of the later craft guilds.

something to justify them in this "reflection." Soon, consciously or unconsciously, this type of *alter ego* becomes a detractor. I am in his way unless goodnaturedly I will let him trade on me. Or in me.

But the individuality of my work has never swerved from first to last. It grows steadily on its own center line. The system, or lack of it—I have never had an "office" in the conventional manner—has become fixed habit and works well enough—but only because I stay directly with it in every detail, myself. When I go away there is usually trouble and sometimes unpremeditated treachery. No. There was never organization in the sense that the usual architect's office knows organization. Nor any great need of it so long as I stood actually at the center of the effort. Where I am, there is my office. My office is me. And therein is one great difference between my own and current practice. A severe and exacting limitation instead of the freedom I intended. . . .

The same formula impressed upon all: not to imagine they were coming to school. They were coming in to make themselves as useful to me as they could. I was an architect at work. . . . Some would soon drop out—unable to stand the too great freedom—abusing it. Some would take it and go away with what they could pick up to sell it as their own. Others would thrive on freedom. A fine loyalty characterized all but very few as they were with me in full freedom of their own choice—entirely on their own.

Well, how about them? What have they accomplished?

The architectural world into which they emerged was wholly commercialized and fashionably if not fatuously inclined now toward the "great" styles. . . . I have had occasion to reproach some of my young men for what seemed to me selling out—going too easily with the current of commercial degeneration. The usual answer was "Mr. Wright, we have to live."

"Why?" I have said.

And I don't see why anyone "has" to live, at any rate not live as a parasite at expense of the thing he loves. Why not try something else . . . ?

Some identified themselves with other movements: "It is so hard to stand alone." Others became competitors, the "also-ran" and no less. . . .

I know all too well the weight of opposition all encountered and I am inclined to sympathize with them. . . . Many of my boys are giving a good account of themselves, Middle-West, North-West, South-West and West, and across the seas. But current life mocks most of our effort forward, breaks it to fragments if it can. . . .

Nevertheless, principle alone is defense and refuge from chaos. Otherwise utter defeat.[12]

12. *Autobiography*, pp. 235-38.

Except for a curious twist, the situation is thoroughly Arthurian. In a land where evil has spread abroad, a band of young knights, all presumably devoted to the cause of truth, gathers around a dauntless warrior. ("Do none of you go into architecture to get a living unless you love architecture as a principle at work, for its own sake—prepared to be true to it as to your mother, your comrade, or yourself." [13]) United by a bond of sympathy and understanding, they work together with loyalty and enthusiasm, regarding each new commission as an opportunity for striking a blow at corruption. There are the Modreds, "some six or seven" who are traitorous at heart; but there exists a threat of dissension and treachery among even the faithful knights when they are not under Arthur's watchful eye. The endurance of the Round Table depends in the last analysis upon him alone, yet it is in the nature of his role and of his personality that he cannot train a successor. The kingship is not an office which the man Arthur happens to fill; Camelot is his personal creation, inconceivable apart from his standing at its center. (Tennyson's Arthur, too, could have said, "My office is me.") One by one the knights must go forth on their own, even as they came, to prove themselves, to fulfill their own destinies. Many are not strong enough and succumb, in one way or another, to the forces of evil; some give a good account of themselves in various corners of the kingdom; no one, however, becomes the new Arthur.

But here we come to the novel variation in the story that makes Wright's position more difficult than Arthur's. In Tennyson's *Idyls,* as Johnson points out, the role of the king is peculiarly passive; the deeds are performed by the knights, rarely by Arthur himself, who stands for a stable principle of collectivity that is contrasted to the dynamic questing of the knights. Wright, however, was at once Arthur and Galahad; he was both symbol of the cause and its chief prosecutor, a fatherly guiding spirit who was himself pursuing the unique self-fulfillment that the quest for the Grail represents.

What made the lot of the Taliesin apprentices harder than that of Camelot's knights was Wright's uncompromising acceptance of a Romantic attitude toward imitation. "According to Voltaire," Irving Babbitt remarks, "genius is only judicious imitation. According to Rous-

13. *Future of Architecture,* pp. 217-18.

seau the prime mark of genius is refusal to imitate."[14] From the beginning Wright had associated the imitation of models with Beaux-Arts academicism and with everything he considered sterile and pernicious in architecture. Art that is not original, he felt, scarcely deserves to be called art. Was it possible, then, for a member of the Fellowship, setting out to make his way in the world, to avoid at once the Scylla of abandoning the Cause and the Charybdis of imitating the master? The Cause was so wholly identified with Wright himself that either the young architect-errant had to break away altogether, whereupon he was reproached for "selling out," or else he practiced what he had learned at Camelot and was charged with plagiarism. Some few managed to sail through the straits, but the way was narrow and the course uncharted. The happiest solution, both for King Arthur and for Wright, was for the young man simply to remain permanently at the palace. Wright did not at all like to see his apprentices leave Taliesin, for in doing so they posed a threat at once to his own pre-eminence and to the solidarity of the brotherhood.

Wright fully understood all this, of course. If he had not been convinced that the Cause was grounded in the nature of Nature itself, and therefore was greater than he and so had to be carried to the whole world, he could not have built the buildings he erected, nor could he have taken on his apprentices in that Cause. He firmly believed that those buildings point to, or are the image of, something that is eternally true and that lies at the very heart of the American tradition. But it was supremely important to him that that something be *his* discovery and that it be embodied in *his* invention, created by *his* thought and *his act* (cf. *Work Song*). We find in all this a better exemplification even than the story of King Arthur of the difficulty Tennyson sought to describe a generation before Wright was born: the dilemma of the Individualist in the service of a Cause.

Wright's idea or image of a dedicated fellowship of believers was based upon a precarious amalgamation of certain aspects of Christian pietism, early monasticism, and Arthurian romance. Like the monk or the aspiring young knight, he who wanted to join the Fellowship had

14. Irving Babbitt, *Rousseau and Romanticism* (Cleveland: The World Publishing Company [Meridian Books], n.d.), p. 41.

to come voluntarily and unbidden, severing his attachment to the traditions in which he had previously been trained. He had to submit himself to a disciplined way of life: "Our home life must be simple. Meals in common. Fixed hours for work, recreation, and sleep. Each worker will have his or her room for study and rest. . . . Each will be required to contribute his or her share of work each day on the grounds or new buildings or on the farm." [15] The reward of that life would lie in a special kind of awakening that was to come to one through this ideal fusion of freedom and participation.

We have noted in passing the kinship between Wright's house at Taliesin and the McCormick project of 1907. Hitchcock opines that the latter would have been "almost like a Persian palace." Taliesin was a palace, too: it was Wright's Camelot, where he was venerated by his young followers no less than was Arthur by his. It exemplified in microcosm, as every well-ordered palace should, the mode of relatedness that was held by its occupants to be the true governance for the nation; it sheltered a miniature society, embracing domesticity, agriculture, industry, and education, and it undertook to show how all these should rightly be integrated into a meaningful, satisfying way of life.

As was the case with Camelot and the monastery, Taliesin comprises a little world that is at once within and over against the *world,* in that sense of the word we associate with the First Epistle of John. In taking for himself the old family motto, "Truth against the World," Wright declared concomitantly that the world is against truth. Whosoever would show forth truth in the world must therefore stand apart from the world and be not conformed to it. (At bottom this is the reason for Wright's failure in Oak Park: he was trying to be a part of the thing he wanted to reshape, so that he had no vantage point of his own.) Hence the image of Camelot, both as a place of retreat from the world and of preparation for attack against the evils of the world, was supremely important to the realization of what Wright felt to be his mission.

I would have you so teach him to know the world [declared Rousseau] that he should think ill of all that takes place in it. Let him know that man is by nature good, let him feel it, let him judge his neighbor by himself;

15. *Autobiography,* pp. 392-94.

but let him see how men are depraved and perverted by society; let him find the source of all their vices in their preconceived opinions; let him be disposed to respect the individual, but to despise the multitude.[16]

This was the doctrine Taliesin was built to defend.

The Fellowship was the expression, furthermore, of an ideal which Wright believed to govern the whole of his architectural practice. Speaking of his relationship to his clients, he says:

So, should a man come to me for a building he would be ready for me. It would be what I could do for him that he wanted. I have opened the door and shown many a man out of my office when I found that he sought mere novelty and did not understand what I would be doing for him. Only the other day it was the name that interested a client. He was not up to this organic endeavor in building, I knew.[17]

It is as if some unworthy candidate had knocked at the gates of Camelot and sought to join the Round Table simply because he was impressed with its fame in the land. In Wright's thinking no less than in Calvin's there is implicit a principle of predestination and of election: those who are fit to join will come without being asked, and only the fit will be admitted. It applied not only to applicants for Taliesin apprenticeship but to everyone who aspired to lead an organic life in organic architecture. Theoretically, at least, every client had to show himself to be a member of that "new and innate aristocracy our humanity needs."

That aristocracy was to be different from those that had supported the architect, and had been supported by architecture, in ages past. It was to be established or defined not in terms of hereditary status or of wealth or of political power, but rather in terms of an *endeavor,* a striving after an ideal. Like the aristocracy of the Round Table, its very existence would depend upon an active spiritual awareness and purposeful intention on the part of its members. For a most apposite expression of the ideal we must go back to Tennyson, who, in a moment of extraordinary insight, recognized about the time Wright was born the nature of that tension between architecture and music that concerned so many people in the nineteenth century and that lay at the

16. *Emile,* p. 198.
17. *Future of Architecture,* pp. 250-51.

very core of Wright's thought and feeling. In *Gareth and Lynette,* which was written in the late 1860s and published in 1872, the young Gareth, approaching Camelot, sees the castle mysteriously emerge and disappear in the mists. Wondering what kind of enchanted place this may be, he asks an old man whom he meets to explain the elusive vision. The man tells him about Camelot and concludes his cryptic exposition with the following words:

> For an ye heard a music, like enow
> They are building still, seeing the city is built
> To music, therefore never built at all,
> And therefore built forever. (ll. 271-74)

Tennyson means, I take it, that the existence of Camelot and of the Order of the Round Table depends upon a state of mind or of personal being rather than upon any sort of "objective" structure—a legal constitution, a body of canonical regulations, an official hierarchy—such as has sustained the kind of state to the service of which architecture has traditionally been devoted. The Round Table is maintained against the disintegration with which the world threatens it in the way music is maintained against the continuous threat of silence and nothingness: by constant exertion, by endeavor. "So far as architecture has gone in my own thought," says Wright, "it is first of all a character and quality of *mind* that may enter also into human conduct with social implications. . . ." [16]

Fallingwater: A Growing Plant

HOWEVER, IF the ethic of the Round Table is to be relevant to the tainted world outside the palace, it must nevertheless be grounded in the essential nature of that world, or else it would be extraneous and arbitrary. The underlying reality that makes the ethic universally valid reveals itself to Wright, as it did to Rousseau and the Romantic poets, in the integrated and organic nature of Nature, with whose order man is naturally or ideally in harmony. Our basic problem is that of rediscovering our natural place in that order of things.

18. *Autobiography,* p. 344.

Wright's chief value-word was "organic." He applied it to details of construction, to single buildings, to kinds of architecture, to ways of living, and to conceptions of society as a whole—and yet he never clearly said what he meant by the word. It had for him the kind of meaning we customarily designate by the word "religious": in general, it pertained to his emotional commitment to certain convictions about man and the world; more specifically it expressed his fundamental belief or intuition about *religio*—about that which makes possible a "binding up," a turning of the many into one—in short, "universe."

In all that pertains to their architecture (or in regard to what their architecture pertains to), the Greeks found a clue to the essential meaning of things in the self-contained, normative, and highly articulated form of the human body. They were committed, by and large, to a kind of visualist thinking that proceeds upon the assumption that complex orders of things, social and otherwise, possess an anatomy that is subject to being analyzed; wherefore they could answer the "religious" question or questions in figural and architectural metaphors that were based upon, or were analogous to, certain of the body's structural and formal characteristics. For Wright, as for most modern painters, the body provided no such clue, and the metaphors derived from it were dead. It was rather in the tree that he found his key to the problem of order.

> Here the promotion of an idea from the material to the spiritual plane began to have consequences. Conceive now that an entire building might grow up out of conditions as a plant grows up out of the soil and yet be free to be itself, to "live its own life according to Man's Nature." Dignified as a tree in the midst of nature but a child of the spirit of man. I now propose an ideal for the architecture of the machine age, for the ideal American building. Let it grow up in that image. The tree. But I do not mean to suggest the imitation of the tree.[19]

Wright did not elaborate upon this proposal or state precisely what the relation of a building to a tree should be, but his meaning is reasonably clear. First of all comes the relation of the tree to the ground. We do not think of a tree as resting heavily upon the ground, as does a block of stone or a Greek temple; instead, it seems at once to

19. *The Natural House*, p. 46.

grip the ground and to rise up from it—to possess its place in a living and dynamic way. "We start with the *ground*. This is rock and *humus*. A building is planted there to survive the elements." [20] Wright said that he would like for each of his houses to look as if it could exist nowhere but in the spot where it stands. For all his praise of Heraclitus and the Law of Change, he was as much concerned as were the builders of the Pyramids with affirming man's permanent possession of a *place* in the world; not however, a place where he can resist every effort at dislodging him, but a natural place that receives him, sustains him, and is wholly in accord with him, even as a tree is united with the spot it clutches. The planted fixity of his houses is no less meaningful than is that of the Medici Palace, but it is of a different kind, depending not upon weight and mass but upon a unique reciprocity between house and site.

A relationship of this sort was first adumbrated in such early works as the Glasner house, was fully achieved at Taliesin in 1911, was enunciated as a general principle in the early 1930s, and found its finest expression in the Kaufmann house of 1936.[21] It is still the critical consensus, I believe, that Fallingwater is Wright's most imaginative realization of his conception of the "natural house," built in Nature for the natural man, who himself "shall be like a tree planted by the rivers of water." If ever a house was rooted in the landscape it is this one.

PLATE XXIII

Another arboreal characteristic that lends itself to metaphorical interpretation is the manner of a tree's growth. Unlike the human body, which reaches its full stature early in the course of its existence, a tree continues to grow as long as it remains alive. One of the aspects of classical art and thought which seemed most reprehensible to Wright was their indifference to the phenomenon of growth. It is equally characteristic of the Parthenon, of Plato's city of 5040 citizens (in the *Laws*), and of Le Corbusier's Apartment for 1600 Persons that they are all sprung fullborn as Athena herself and do not admit the possibility of growth or expansion. For Wright, on the other hand,

20. *Future of Architecture,* p. 298.

21. It may be objected, of course, that Fallingwater was not a family home at all, but only a weekend lodge or retreat for a couple whose only son was no longer living at home. This, I think, is irrelevant. As I suggested in Chapter 1, all of Wright's houses are best understood as "self-portraits." The problems he wrestles with are his own, not his clients'. . . .

Modern architecture is a natural architecture—the architecture of nature, for Nature. . . . If pattern is to be made at all, it must be free pattern, the one most suited to growth, the one most likely to encourage and concede growth to life. That means, I think, the end of the word "institution" as we have set it up.[22]

Here, in effect, is the charge that Wright made against his family in 1909: it had ceased to "concede growth" to his life.

Since a building does not grow, the idea must be expressed, as Wright indicates, in its structural patterns, which in turn must reveal the nature of the institution for which the building is erected. The crux of the matter lies in the relation of part to part and of part to whole. Wright asserts that these relationships should not seem fixed, governed (as in the Doric order) by an invariant regulatory principle, but should rather possess something of the flexibility and self-transforming vitality of a growing plant.

One might suppose that Wright's conception of the organic, bound up as it is with his attitudes toward the community, would show some kinship with the organismic theories of society which were much in vogue among a number of nineteenth-century sociologists. Such is not the case, however; for, like John of Salisbury, they based their organic analogies upon the human body. In his *Polycraticus* (1159) John likened the state to a body of which the prince is the head, the senate is the heart, the soldiers are the hands, the fiscal officers are the stomach and intestines, and the peasants are the feet. Whether in John's hands or in those of Lilienfeld and Novikov seven hundred years later, the analogy was invariably employed in defense of the corporate state, with its citizenry ordered into a hierarchy of specialized classes, even as the body is composed of differentiated and specialized organs. At the top of the hierarchy stands an aristocratic elite, corresponding to the brain, which alone is able to direct the operation of the body as a whole.

But if one were to base his analogy upon one of the higher forms of plant life, such as a tree, one would find no basis whatever for corporate distinctions. The tree has a much larger number of parts than the human body, but a smaller number of kinds of part. It sprouts from the ground as a leaf-bearing twig, whereafter for decades, even

22. *Ibid.*, p. 248.

for centuries, it grows and expands in every direction, adapts itself to the conditions of its site and environment, develops in ways that cannot be predicted and that make each tree unique in form, but remains to the end only an elaboration of the simple twig-structure of the original seedling. The tree shapes itself so as to get as many leaves as possible up into the sunlight; yet it has no brain, no member that directs or members that are directed. It is stable, enduring, self-sufficient, unaggressive; it exists simply in order to realize itself in a continuous life-process of growth and expansion.

By pointing to the tree rather than to the body, Wright found justification in nature for an organic society without organs—that is, without specialized classifications, groupings, and functions. The incorporation of the parts is of a different order: as Wright liked to put it, "The part is to the whole as the whole is to the part." The member does not exist in order to serve the family, nor the citizen to serve the state; nor are the family and the state simply service institutions which have no other purpose than to provide for the all-important individual. The family is rather a grouping which makes possible a meaningful existence for the single person by affording him membership and a *place*—a natural and unconstrained place, as in the openness of the sunlit natural world. The tree resembles the family and the state in that it has the power to endure and to produce generation after generation of leaves; yet the leaf remains the creative and productive element upon which the life of the tree wholly depends.

Once again we find Wright's thought conservative and of-a-piece with the Romantic tradition. Hoxie Fairchild points out, in *The Romantic Quest,* that nature was conceived in the eighteenth century to be like a watch, while in the nineteenth century it was thought to be like a tree, "at once vast and intimate, . . . free, plastic, and expansive, rather than determined, final, and restrictive." [23] Goethe, too, was preoccupied with such matters. In his later years he was fascinated by the study of plants, especially the succulent *bryophyllum calycinum,* of which a severed leaf, when partially covered with wet sand, will put forth roots and produce an independent plant. The phenomenon

23. Hoxie N. Fairchild, *The Romantic Quest* (Philadelphia: A. Saifer, 1931), p. 10.

aroused in Goethe the greatest excitement and led him to declare, "All is leaf, and through this singleness the greatest multiplicity becomes possible."

Plainly Goethe was not passionately stirred by the scientific observation that a few kinds of leaf will take root in moist stand. The vast majority will not, so there is no general biological principle involved. It was rather that in this oddity he found a metaphor: nature's declaration, so to speak, both of the ultimate primacy of the individual and of the organic continuity between the individual and the larger society of which he is product and member. He found to reside in the single leaf the "total planthood" (*Allpflanzenschaft*) of the species. Even though the leaf might not in the least resemble the many-membered plant, Goethe was convinced that the nature of the species as a whole is completely embodied in every part of the organism. His leaf metaphor, like Wright's tree metaphor, purports to demonstrate that "the part is to the whole as the whole is to the part."

Wright's finest expression of the idea is to be found in the Kaufmann house. The building is composed of thousands of simple rectangles, ranging in size from stones no larger than a man's hand to seventy-foot concrete parapets. These similar and unspecialized units are grouped together into larger components of many sizes, some vertical, some horizontal; yet neither the component group nor the house as a whole is rectangular in shape. The building presents many different and irregular silhouettes to the moving observer, but always the shape seems to respond to the site. Above the stream it is composed of long, quiet horizontals; over the jutting ledges that drop away beside the waterfall it is made up of short, ledgy projections; and toward the rocky hillside that rises steeply behind the house it raises a vertical masonry face with relatively few breaks. It seems to spring like a low shrub from its craggy foothold, to cling, bare and sparse on one side, to the ground that supports it, and to spread itself upward and outward on the other, into the air and the sunlight.

In classical and medieval buildings the shape of a given part is indicative of its function: columns, capitals, bases, lintels, gables, and buttresses are all formed according to their roles in the working structure, even as are the hand, tooth, femur, and knee-cap of a man. In Fallingwater such differentiations scarcely exist—yet not because one shape is made to serve many purposes, but rather because the number of discernible functions had been reduced to the barest minimum, or even because the very notion of functional differentiation has been declared irrelevant. One is not made conscious of the relation of load to support, nor can one readily isolate and identify such nameable parts as roofs, windows, walls, doors, and chimneys. The service of the part to the whole is, as an organizational principle, dispensed with.

As we noted in the second chapter, Wright did not like the phrase "form follows function" but preferred another, "form and function are one." It seemed clear to him that the leaf does not exist to serve the tree nor the tree to serve the leaf. In the living and growing oneness of the tree, within itself and in its responsive relationship to its environment, he found the perfect metaphorical image of what he regarded as the right way—the organic way—of making one out of many, and thereby of ordering the universe, society at large, and the institution of the family.

One feels no desire to name or classify the parts of Fallingwater. The word and the name seem as irrelevant to Wright's house as they are to the experiencing of music. Looking at the house is like hearing a complex piece of music, moreover, in that one never succeeds in grasping the entire pattern at once, as one does that of the Parthenon or of Plato's state. The pattern unfolds gradually as one walks around and about and through the building, discovering new vistas, new rhythmic patterns, and new phrase-like groupings of its innumerable parts, all of which have the simple and noncommittal uniformity of individual notes of music. It is especially in the quality of this temporal experience, coupled with the openness and apparent extensibility of the house, that the idea of growth and change comes to be associated with Wright's static image. The experience is dynamic and exhilarating to an extraordinary degree.

It was observed in the second chapter, that an essential feature of the Hebrew-romantic kind of thinking to which Wright was committed is its conception of the primacy of personal being as contrasted to the being of things. Now the being of objects is the kind we most readily grasp by visual perception; for sight, as Paul Tillich has noted, is the most *objectifying* of our senses. "It is astounding," writes Boman, "how far clear thinking depended for the Greeks upon the visual faculty. . . .

Bruno Snell calls the Greeks *Augenmenschen.* . . . Gunnar Rudberg says of Plato that he 'is a man of sight, of seeing. His thinking is thinking with the eyes, proceeding from what is seen.' "[24] One of the most striking characteristics of the Parthenon is its total amenability to visual cognition: its form, its nature as an object, can be comprehended almost instantaneously from a single point of view. In this respect it might be called idolatrous, from the Hebrew standpoint, no less than the statue of the goddess inside it: it affirms something about the sufficiency of rational comprehension and the primacy of object-being that would have seemed to the author of the second commandment to border on blasphemy. By contrast, one finds it almost impossible ever to grasp Fallingwater as an object. One comes to know it through so varied a succession of experiences that even after prolonged study one finds it difficult to describe accurately or to draw from memory a given aspect of the building. Let me emphasize once more, however, that the experience is not for its own sake; it constitutes a metaphor concerning the fluid, dynamic, and personal nature of the life of the family, which cannot be equated with or symbolized by a simple *object* of any kind whatever.

I find it hard to imagine that Fallingwater will ever come to look old or to stand as an historic monument of a past period, as do the Arch of Titus and the Cathedral of Durham. Many works of modern architecture, including some of Wright's, already appear dated; the house at Bear Run, not at all. That this will always be true no one can say, but Fallingwater seems to hold the promise, at least, of preserving its "presentness" as well as does an Elizabethan madrigal or a Mozart quartet. Like an early Cubist painting, it arouses one to an acute awareness of his own immediate experience rather than presenting itself, in all its otherness, as an enduring object for his contemplation. It is in this above all that its musicality lies. "Teach him to live," declares Rousseau, "rather than to avoid death; life is not breath, but action, the use of our senses, our mind, our faculties, every part of ourselves which makes us conscious of our being."[25]

24. Boman, *Hebrew Thought Compared with Greek,* p. 56.
25. *Emile,* p. 10.

Wright was well aware of the relation of his work to music, and therefore to that special quality of timelessness to which Tennyson calls our attention in *Gareth and Lynette*. Speaking of the music of Beethoven, Wright avows that

once organic character is achieved in the work of Art, that work is forever. Like sun, moon, and stars, great trees, flowers and grass it *is* and stays on while and wherever man is. Other musicians have this mastery also, and greatly, but none I understand so well, none so rich in the abstract idiom of Nature as he—whose portrait Meredith drew in the sentence: "The hand of the wind was in his hair; he seemed to hear with his eyes." [26]

To hear with his eyes! Meredith's is an extraordinary metaphor, pointing to the fact that Beethoven was not an *Augenmensch*—was not given to that Hellenic objectification we associate with both a classic and a scientistic architecture. A number of writers have suggested that Wright's work in the 1930s was influenced or shaped in some measure by the aesthetic of the International Style (Oud, Le Corbusier, Gropius, et al.) I see little evidence of it in the forms themselves and none whatever in their expressive implications. Le Corbusier said once that everything he knew about architecture he had learned while spending three weeks on the Acropolis in Athens. He was an "eye man"; Wright was not.

In Fallingwater the "living room" quality I spoke of earlier now permeates every detail of the design, while "dining room" formality is wholly absent. The house celebrates a mode of familial relatedness that is based upon a lively process of interaction rather than upon an architectonic pattern of orderly submission. We have here Wright's best expression of the ideal that first became fully clear to him when he and Mamah Borthwick established their unconventional household at Taliesin in 1911—a household away from the city, sustained entirely by mutual endeavor and without benefit of law or custom or ceremony. As Rousseau had declared,

The wise man needs no laws. The very words *obey* and *command* will be excluded from his vocabulary, still more those of *duty* and *obligation*. . . .

26. *Autobiography*, p. 423.

When our natural tendencies have not been interfered with by human prejudices and human institutions, the happiness alike of children and of men consists in the enjoyment of their liberty.[27]

In the rugged Bear Run ravine Wright found a site which, like that of Taliesin, afforded him the means of resolving the difficulty he had posed for himself in Oak Park in declaring that there should be as many kinds of house as there are kinds of person. Not only did the structure of the city make for conformity; so did the flat and featureless expanse of the prairie. His early enthusiasm for the prairie is related to his early optimism about the possibilities of the gridiron suburb: at best it made for a judicious compromise between freedom and convention. In exploiting the utter uniqueness of Bear Run, on the other hand, Wright could declare that there is a *natural* basis for radical differentiation.

But what of the matter of agreement? Is it not implied, since the house could exist only here, that my place is not interchangeable with your place, and that therefore there can be no common agreement between us? But no; nature is ultimately one. Even though no two places are alike, all places are on the *ground*. "While man was true to earth," said Wright, "his architecture was creative." [28] Men's natures may be as various as is the earth's terrain; yet there is a "general human personality," as Whitman said, that makes for universal harmony and understanding, even as all places are joined in the unity of Nature. Wordsworth's solitary reaper experiences nothing whatever of the alienation that a Munch or a Kafka knows, for she participates in that harmony, even as does the Taoist sage or Bellini's St. Francis. Wright was confident that this relationship between man and Nature is an essential one, and that its realization in practice would usher in a new harmony among men.

The Johnson Building: The Gospel of Work

In Taliesen, Fallingwater, the Pew house, the Affleck house, and many others, Wright set forth this image of the structural basis of the natural freedom in Nature of a man and his family. In all of them there is

27. *Emile*, pp. 49-53.
28. *Future of Architecture*, p. 34.

realized an idea that was expressed only partially and equivocally in such early works as the Robie and Coonley houses, which were still enmeshed in the fixed patterns of the city.

But what becomes now of the city? What happens to the concern that found expression in the Winslow façade, Unity Temple, and the Robie dining room? Is the old tension between opposites resolved and laid to rest in Fallingwater? Not in the least! Wright's preoccupation with the meaning and value of loyalty, participation, and membership remained as great as it had ever been. Although he occasionally described himself as an advocate of "ruralism," his love for the city and for all it represents as a symbol of collective understanding did not diminish and may even have increased in his later years. His enthusiasm for designing large public buildings for city sites and city purposes was fully equal to his zeal in the cause of decentralization. In fact, his often fanciful urban projects, such as the Steel Cathedral, the Point Park scheme for Pittsburgh, and the Mile High Illinois for Chicago, imply the existence of a greater measure of agreement and of common purpose among the citizenry than was actually there. They are affirmations in favor of coming together that are, in their way, just as powerful as his residential avowals in favor of dispersal.

Perhaps for the very reason that they are visionary images of an agreement that does not exist, none of these grandiose urban projects has been built, or is ever likely to be. Of his executed works, the one that expresses most perfectly this aspect of his conviction is the S. C. Johnson & Company administration building in Racine, which was begun in the same year as the Kaufmann house. The two buildings are in many respects diametrically opposite in character. Fallingwater is composed of a great many distinct parts, while the Johnson building is mostly contained within a single molded, flowing wall. The former has projecting members that extend outward in every direction, giving the building a highly irregular silhouette, while the latter is extraordinarily compact and, to use Wright's own word for it, monolithic. Whereas the house is so open as to appear wall-less, the office building is closed within windowless and unbroken masonry. Fallingwater is cantilevered in such a way that it appears to hover without

PLATE XXVII

adequate support over the Bear Run ravine, while the Johnson building is planted on heavy foundations and contains a much larger number of columnar supports than is structurally necessary.

Indeed, the dissimilarities are so marked that one is tempted to try to explain them in terms of the specific architectural exigencies with which Wright was faced in each of these undertakings. One quickly discovers, however, that there are no functional considerations pertaining either to domesticity or to business administration that make these particular forms necessary. It is plain to see that both block-like houses and glass-walled office buildings are vastly more numerous than are buildings like these two, both of which seem somewhat eccentric within the general context of mid-twentieth-century American architecture. In both cases, I believe, the eccentricities can be accounted for only in terms of the human issues with which the architect was concerned.

The most topical of the problems to which the Johnson building addresses itself bears upon the experience of working, or of having a job—a matter with which almost everyone was concerned during the Depression, the effects of which were still everywhere evident in 1936. Ubiquitous joblessness must have made it apparent to many sensitive persons that in our modern world the threat whose meaning most nearly approximates that of banishment and excommunication is, as Tillich has observed, that of unemployment. It is especially true of the white-collar office worker (for whom the Johnson building was designed) that he tends to think of his job as his "position." Humbler persons may have only a "place," but to lose one's "position" is to suffer a grievous loss of social status and of psychological security—as indeed it is in some degree for every worker, since to be unemployed is to be useless and unneeded, to have no place in the great productive enterprise that constitutes the very fabric of the American social organism and embodies, as did the church in the Middle Ages, all its aspirations toward betterment (aspirations that are almost universally expressed, in our society, in terms of the "rising standard of living" which the enterprise holds out to us as a kind of progressive salvation). Just as the possibility of excommunication charges with meaning the great doors and sheltering interior of the cathedral, or the possibility of banishment, the tightly contrived membering of the Parthenon, so the danger of unemployment lends meaning to the embracing walls of the office building at Racine.

PLATE XXV

PLATE XXVI

Wright had first become aware of the possibilities of the commercial building when he designed the offices of the Larkin Company in 1904. What with its simplicity, severity, and symmetrical formality, that structure fits easily enough into the sizable class of Wright's public edifices that was discussed in the third chapter. Yet when we compare it with the club houses and apartment buildings from that decade, we see that it possesses an imposing dignity the others generally lack. In part this is due to its size (it is the largest of Wright's early works); but equally important is the framing of the block by the great windowless double pylons—the first about ninety, the second about a hundred feet high—which stood at its four corners. While vertical corner elements of this sort are fairly common in Wright's work prior to 1910, there is only one other structure in which they are used to produce an effect comparable to what we see here—namely, Unity Temple, which was designed in the following year. The kinship between the two buildings is unmistakable.

PLATE XXIV

The Larkin Company had been founded in the 1870s by John Larkin and his idealistic brother-in-law, Elbert Hubbard. By comparison with the general run of commercial firms at the turn of the century, it was a model of business progressivism. By 1904 Hubbard had retired from it and had become completely absorbed in his Roycroft ventures in nearby East Aurora. He was still closely connected with the firm by family ties, however, for two of its officers were married to his sisters. While Larkin went on to build up a mail-order business that eventually employed over five thousand persons and was capitalized at thirty million dollars, Hubbard devoted himself, under the influence of William Morris, to a program of agriculture, handicrafts, and education.

Apparently it was in Buffalo, then, that Wright first found an opportunity to express in architectural form his growing conviction concerning the ethical and organizational significance of industrial enterprise in the modern world. In his 1908 article he described the Larkin building as having been designed to "house the commercial engine of the Larkin Company," and asserted that "the work may have the same claim to consideration as a 'work of art' as an ocean liner, a locomotive or a battleship." [29] For the doctrinaire functionalist of the 1930s this would have meant that the Larkin building was as admirable as those great machines because its forms were determined, as were theirs, by pragmatic considerations of function and economy. I suspect, however, that Wright's choice of these three examples was dictated by something more than his admiration for their straightforward efficiency. The three have two things in common: each is enormously powerful, and each either contains within itself or is directly bound up with an intricate but single-purposed social organism, the dynamic cohesiveness of which stands in sharpest contrast to the casual loose-jointedness we find expressed in Taliesin and Fallingwater. The choice was determined, that is, by the architect's conception of the Larkin Company as a "commercial engine"—an idea that has to do with the productive activity of a large number of collaborating employees, not with the structural efficiency of the building itself.

In selecting photographs of the Larkin building for his 1908 article, Wright confined his choice, as other authors have not, to those made from the ground rather than from the windows of adjacent buildings. That is to say, he chose only those in which there is a marked effect of perspective loom—an effect that lends the building a dynamism of the sort we commonly associate with photographs of great ships taken from a nearby position at water level. (The word "nave" comes to mind as being applicable to both the exterior and interior aspects of the building.) However, the structure itself has no formal characteristics that would remind one of either a vessel or a locomotive. The Johnson building, on the other hand, is streamlined throughout. It does not resemble a ship or a car, but its shapes are of the kind we associate with modern high-speed transportation. A thoroughgoing functionalist would argue, of course, that streamlining is as irrelevant to an office building as it is to an electric iron or a kitchen mixer. Certainly it added greatly to the expense of construction, necessitating the manufacture of bricks in some two hundred different shapes. But such a conclusion is like deciding that it would have been more practical for the Athenians to have built the Parthenon without columns.

29. "In the Cause of Architecture," 1908, pp. 166-67.

The aspirations of present-day Americans, in contrast to those of the Greeks, are forward-looking and progressivistic in character; and certainly no symbol of progressive modernity more appeals to the popular imagination in our time than the streamlined shape; no symbol of personal success and well-being surpasses the possession of a rakish new car. (Wright's own enthusiasm for fast cars was of legendary proportions.) It is with such shapes that the unspoken hopes, dreams, and desires of millions of American citizens are associated, and it was by appealing to those almost universal aspirations, it would seem, that Wright sought to make his building an effective symbol of agreement in that troubled era when the very word "corporation" had taken on an opprobrious meaning for millions of people. As it had been the purpose of the cathedral builder, in the midst of the violence, heresy, and inquisitorial persecution of the thirteenth century (cf. Luchaire's *Social History*), to erect a compelling symbol of the church's power to unify and to stabilize, so it was Wright's purpose in 1936 to proclaim the power of the industrial establishment to bring men together in peaceful and productive collaboration.

In his Oak Park years Wright had delighted in the cultivated leisure of urban life and had indulged himself and his family in every kind of luxury; but now in the 1930s he declared himself to be a preacher of "the unpopular gospel of Work." Unsympathetic to the giantism of corporate management and the hostile attitudes of organized labor, as well as to an increasingly bureaucratic government's conception of "relief," he reaffirmed the religious significance of work—that is to say, its potentiality for binding together a factious and fractured society. Once more his reaction was to turn back to the ideals of Emerson and Carlyle.

> Properly speaking [wrote the latter] all true Work is Religion: and whatsoever Religion is not Work may go and dwell among the Brahmins, Antinomians, Spinning Dervishes, or where it will; with me it shall have no harbour. Admirable was that of the old Monks, "*Laborare est Orare,* Work is Worship." Older than all preached Gospels was this unpreached, inarticulate, but ineradicable, forever-enduring Gospel: Work, and therein have wellbeing. . . . All true Work is sacred. . . .[30]

30. Carlyle, *Past and Present,* Book 3, Chap. 12.

Work is worship—but what kind of worship? One to which the Romantics were strongly attracted: *liturgical* worship. It may at first glance seem surprising that this was the case (one might have expected them to incline toward something closer to glossolalia); but liturgy is the polar counterpart of that personal emotionality which the Romantics in so many ways cultivated. (One thinks of the attraction that was felt by the latter-day Romantics of the 1930s toward communism and surrealism simultaneously.) The word itself goes back to the Greek word *leitourgia* (leitos = public, from leos = people, plus ergo = to do), which designated certain kinds of public service. The route by which the early Christians passed from the joyous bread-breaking of the *agape*, or love-feast, to the liturgical worship of an established church cannot be traced in detail; but it was the same route which brought them to the point of being willing, in the fourth century, both to accept state sponsorship and to support the program and the pretensions of the state. It was only at this point that the church came to need the state-related institutional symbols that the art of architecture alone can provide.

"Liturgy implies a communal life, and a communal life that is solidly organized, to which the individual must adapt himself without question." [31] The quintessential ideal of the liturgical church in the Middle Ages was expressed in the institution of monasticism. Amidst the political breakdown of the Dark Age the monasteries of western Europe kept alive a Roman conception of lawful government, of a disciplined and regulated society, solidly organized and demanding the unquestioning submission of its members. The central structure of the monastic community was a hypostyle church that was descended from the public halls that had housed the law courts of the Roman state.

It was suggested above that industrial employment fulfills a need in our society comparable to the one that was satisfied by membership in the medieval church or the ancient *polis*. Wright meant to express this at Racine: "Organic architecture designed this great building to

31. Joseph A. Jungman, S.J., *The Early Liturgy* (Notre Dame, Indiana: University of Notre Dame Press, 1959), p. 10.

be as inspiring a place to work as any cathedral ever was in which to worship."[32] Work is liturgy—a form of public service, the essence of one's participation in the community.

For the American liberal of the 1930s, who put his faith in heavy industrialization under governmental regulation and in the bellicose campaign of the CIO, Wright's attitude toward industrial employment and industrial peace could only be described as reactionary in the extreme. And indeed, by comparison with his earlier work, the Johnson building does, for all its streamlined modernity, reveal a conservative reaction on its architect's part. It is not hard to perceive, and to find meaning in, the cathedral-like character of the twin-towered façades and the unified, vertical, seven-bayed interior of the Larkin building, the design of which Wright himself adapted almost immediately to the needs of a church. The Johnson building has it pair of towers, also; but though they flank the entrance of a perfectly symmetrical structure, they cannot be seen as part of a public façade. Ostensibly the design of the covered, interior entrance was determined by considerations having to do with the automobile and its parking; but it was not necessary that the building should present a blank masonry wall to the street, or that the entrance and parking lot should be located at the center and rear of the building site. The elimination of the street façade and the new handling of the doorway are part and parcel of a general change in character that separates the Johnson from the Larkin offices. If we can detect in the massive verticality of the earlier building some resemblance to a cathedral, perhaps we can see in the later one, what with its pervasive suggestions of closure and withdrawal, an approximation to the monastery. Whereas the Gothic cathedral ordinarily adjoined the market place and extended its great portrals invitingly to the secular world, the monastery was typically set apart from that world and stood more or less against it.

We noted earlier that Wright's conception of the Taliesin Fellowship was quasi-monastic in character, and that the idea had come to him partly, it would seem, by way of Elbert Hubbard's cooperative community (Manson calls it "monkish") at East Aurora. In the 1890s "Fra Elbertus," as he liked to be called, had launched a protest against

32. *Autobiography,* p. 472.

what he regarded as the degrading industrialism of that day. In the early 1900s, when Hubbard's success was at its height, Wright had assumed a deliberately opposite and, as he saw it, radically modern position by declaring himself the champion of the "art and craft of the machine." It was at this point that he designed the Larkin building, as a positive affirmation in favor of an industrialization which seemed to him full of promise for the future. (Its proximity to East Aurora and its relationship to Hubbard and his family may have given Wright a good deal of slightly malicious satisfaction.)

In the 1930s, on the other hand, it was he himself who had become an outspoken opponent of the prevailing situation, even as Hubbard had been decades earlier. He was not opposed to mechanization, however, but rather to the "superconcentrations" of power and of people in corporations which, he thought, were so out of scale with the human being as to threaten with annihilation the "human-element" in the worker's existence. "Democracy," he then declared, "must be an integrated society of small units."

Mr. Johnson's wax business was of roughly the same size as had been Mr. Larkin's mail-order business in 1904; but whereas the Larkin Company had been a typical American enterprise in the early 1900s, the Johnson Company—small-town, family-controlled, paternalistic and anti-union in policy—was decidedly unlike the giant corporations that dominated the industrial world of 1936. Wright's building, then, is not a "cathedral of labor," positively affirming its congenial relation to the market place; it avows, instead, the separate and self-contained nature of this community of workers, dedicated to the defense of an ideal to which the world at large was increasingly hostile.[33] Its relationship to Taliesin, which also involved a withdrawal from the world on the part of an intimate fellowship of co-workers, is self-evident. Indeed,

33. I am reminded in this connection of the Johnson Wax Company's Christmas television program of 1956, in the course of which the robed members of the company choir, carrying candles and singing hymns, were shown making their way around the galleries and down the spiral stairways of the administration building. One would scarcely expect to find a company choir in the Seagram Building, say, or in the General Motors Technical Center; and certainly it would occur to no one to present either of those buildings in the guise of a monastic church. Wright's building lends itself to such presentation very well indeed.

as one would expect to be the case at the "palace," where the image of ideal governance is set forth, Taliesin has its own "great workroom"—viz., the large draughting room, articulated not with columns but with a multitude of triangular supports, which was built only a year or so before the Johnson building. In both cases the working members of the institution are gathered among the working members of the building itself.

What I am concerned to establish in all this is the relationship of the Johnson building, in both form and meaning, to the church (be it monastic or otherwise) and to a long tradition of civic and religious architecture that goes back far beyond the advent of Christianity. For it is of the greatest importance to observe that the Johnson building is the finest example of the hypostyle hall in twentieth-century architecture.

Despite the fact that the word "hypostyle" means *under* columns, most modern persons, following Schopenhauer and the functionalists, tend to think of the column in relation to what is above it, or to the load it carries. The ancients, on the other hand, knew that the principal element in those halls is the *floor*. It was upon the floor plane that members of the community came together periodically in order to reaffirm their common agreement—or their common *understanding*, as we sometimes put it, in a word that reveals in itself the connection between agreement and the possession of a place that is held in common; for if I say I understand you, I mean that I can stand where you stand, or that we share the same "standpoint." It was upon the communal floor, then, that the interchangeable columns stood, working together to maintain a sheltering and enduring structure that was the chief symbol of the body politic.

Although pillared and columniated halls are to be found in a number of modern factories and department stores, I know of no instance in which the form is used in a way that is so nearly comparable, both visually and metaphorically, to the familiar ways of ancient and medieval building. Le Corbusier was responsive to the column as symbol and employed colonnades of one kind or another in many of his buildings; yet his imagination inclined always toward a stark and radical abstraction, so that his ranks of *pilotis* and his colonnaded halls do not evoke the sense of warm and lively participation that the Johnson workroom arouses. For this is a space in which people are encouraged to think of themselves as members, united upon a common floor in a common understanding, even as were the citizens of Rome in the Basilica Ulpia or the members of the early church in Old St. Peter's.

Shortly after the completion of the administration building Wright was commissioned to design another structure to house the Johnson Company's research laboratories. Though not compelled to do so by lack of space, the architect chose to erect a square tower that would be the tallest building in Racine. Whatever resemblance the original edifice may have borne to a monastery was greatly increased by this addition—though of course the similarity is one Wright may not have been conscious of. Throughout the latter part of his life he was strongly attracted to the tower from as an urban symbol (e.g., Steel Cathedral, St. Mark's Tower, Price Tower, the Mile High Illinois). While the form was evidently associated in his mind with that sense of "power and authority" that had so appealed to Nietzsche, we cannot fully know what the tower meant to him. For that matter, however, we do not know what it meant to the medieval monk. Some monastic towers may have held a few bells, but that alone would scarcely explain the great size and formal complexity of the innumerable structures that are so distinctive a feature of Romanesque architecture. Possibly there is inherent in the form of the tower a powerful ethical symbol that derives from the vertical stance of the human body itself—an aspect of the human condition that puts uprightness on the side of life, strength, aspiration, and well-being, and in opposition to downwardness, defeat, degradation, destruction, despair, and death. Surely it is in keeping with the progressivistic philosophy to which the streamlining of the Johnson building apparently refers that its soaring tower should be devoted to research.

It seems reasonably certain that all ancient and medieval hypostyle halls are descended in one way or another from the king's house and are expressions of a theory of the state that requires the submission of the individual to the demands of the society and its ruler. They bespeak the necessity of conformity in the interests of stability and security; they reflect a more or less pessimistic view of the human condition—a view that persisted at least until the time of Hobbes, who believed that organized societies arose in order that men might be protected from one another. In the following century, however, which saw the institution of kingship challenged and shaken as never before, Rousseau found the origins of society to lie in men's need to share in and benefit from one another's productivity.

> Given ten men, each of them has ten different requirements. To get what he needs for himself each must work at ten different trades; but considering our different talents, one will do better at this trade, another at that. . . . Let us form these ten men into a society, and let each devote himself to the trade for which he is best adapted, and let him work at it for himself and for the rest. . . . This is the plain foundation of all our institutions.[34]

It is to the celebration of this ideal of fruitful collaboration, voluntarily undertaken, that Wright's hypostyle hall is dedicated.

In the Middle Ages and the Renaissance the building of columniated halls was the prerogative of the state-sponsored and state-sponsoring church. For the present-day American church, divorced as it is from the state and responsible no longer for the basic *religio* that makes possible the binding together of the society, the form may well be meaningless. The agency that is now able to bring together people from all levels of the community and to provide for them a meaningful experience of membership, not only within a local organization but within the society at large, is, as we have already suggested, the industrial or commercial establishment. Especially in the United States has this new relationship been realized—witness the following statement by a young Dutchman studying merchandizing in an American department store: "The most astonishing thing about the store is the teamwork. Everybody tries to help everybody else. In Europe, everybody is for himself, and who cares about the other people? . . . Here an executive says with a friendly face to a cleaning woman, 'Hi, Dorothy.' And workers at the store say 'Cubby' to the executive vice president."[35] It was one of the great feats of Wright's imagination to recognize that this genial kind of relationship was a distinctive potentiality of American commerce, and to adapt the ancient form of the hypostyle hall to the purposes and to the style-sense of modern commercial architecture. Unfortunately, the ideal it defends was already a lost cause, so far as the organization of major industries is concerned, before the Johnson building was ever begun.

34. *Emile,* p. 156.
35. *St. Louis Post-Dispatch,* November 13, 1962, p. 3D.

Broadacre City

THE FOURTH of Wright's major accomplishments in the 1930s was the publication of his plan for Broadacre City. The scheme was first sketched out in *The Disappearing City* (1932), was set forth as a concise proposal in an article in the *Architectural Record* in 1935, was summarized in *Architecture and Modern Life* (1938), and was finally expanded into *The Living City* (1958).

What Wright sought to define was a new kind of city, in which the formal opposition of city and country would be eliminated and all the benefits of both city and country life made available to everyone. Actually it was not a plan for a city at all but rather for a rebuilding of the entire nation, a renovation of the state. According to Wright, the primary political unit should be the county; neither city nor state governments, one gathers, are necessary. Each county would have a population density of about one person per acre; so that if the land were uniformly arable, it would be possible to install the present population of the United States in an area only slightly larger than the state of Texas. Most families in Broadacres would live on small farms, ranging in size ordinarily from one to ten acres, though possibly up to as many as forty. For those with no taste for agriculture there would be tall apartment buildings, similar to the Price Tower in Bartlesville, scattered about the landscape. Each farmhouse would be out of sight and earshot of its neighbors, and each family would be "not relatively but absolutely self-sufficient"—though it is stipulated that the farm-dwelling citizen will do part-time work in a small, nearby factory, thereby experiencing the mutuality that was just as important to Wright as "absolute" self-sufficiency.

Facilities for transportation would be highly developed so as to minimize the difficulties incurred by decentralization and dispersal. However, the need for mass transportation would be greatly reduced, in comparison with our present society, since "all common interests take place in a simple coordination wherein all are employed: *little* farms, *little* homes for industry, *little* factories, *little* schools, a *little* university going to the people mostly by way of their interest in the ground, *little* laboratories on their own ground for professional men."[36] As many facilities as possible, that is, would be brought down to the local level and distributed as widely as possible throughout the inhabited area.

Wright does not propound an explicit theory of property ownership for Broadacres. He asserts, on the one hand, that the land allotments will be held on the basis of "use and improvements," all allotments being made by the state and reverting to the state if not worked directly by the persons to whom they are made, so that there can be no control of the land by a rentier class. But on the other hand, "with his feet on his own ground each man is not only a potential but an actual capitalist."[37] Since every family would be at least relatively self-sufficient, there would be no proletariat, subject to exploitation by a class of owners. Differences in economic status would continue to exist: there would be minimum, medium, and luxurious homes (distinguished most obviously by the number of cars their garages would accommodate); but "quality is in all, for all, alike. What differs is only individuality and extent. There is nothing poor or mean in Broadacres."[38] Although Wright proposed that public utilities be owned by the community, he allowed that the small industrial plants would be in private hands—not so much because he believed in the intrinsic merit of private ownership, it would seem, as because state ownership would bring about a "superconcentration" of economic power, or at least a mammoth industrial bureaucracy, both of which he abhorred.

Wright had nothing whatever to say about the political strategies that would be relied upon to bring all this about. Sometimes he professed to believe that the development of our society, for all its misshapen ugliness, is leading inevitably toward Broadacres, wherefore there is no political problem involved.

The three major inventions already at work building Broadacres, whether the powers that over-built the old cities otherwise like it or not are:
(1) The motor car: general mobilization of the human being.

36. Frank Lloyd Wright, "Broadacre City: a New Community Plan," *Architectural Record,* LXXVII (April 1935), 247.

37. Baker Brownell and Frank Lloyd Wright, *Architecture and Modern Life* (New York: Harper & Row, Publishers, Inc., 1938), p. 309.

38. "Broadacre City: a New Community Plan," p. 246.

(2) Radio, telephone and telegraph: electrical intercommunication becoming complete.
(3) Standardized machine-shop production: machine invention plus scientific discovery.[39]

Needless to say, Wright does not explain just how or why this universal mechanization will lead to the total "organicization" of society; one might logically have supposed that he would have thought the opposite: that the machine and the tree are incommensurate and irreconcilable.

The whole of his political program is summed up in the declaration that all that is required for the realization of the new city is our being allowed

to exercise the use of three inherent rights of any man:
(1) His social right to a direct medium of exchange in place of gold as a commodity: some form of social credit.
(2) His social right to his place on the ground as he has had it in the sun and air: land to be held only by use and improvements.
(3) His social right to the ideas by which and for which he lives: public ownership of inventions and scientific discoveries that concern the life of the people.[40]

Not only these rights but also the nonhistorical and naïve conception of social change that underlies Wright's proposal stem from a tradition of socialist, anarchist, and utopian thought that takes us back on the one hand to a series of popular literary works (to Mary Griffith's *Three Hundred Years Hence,* 1836; to Sylvester Judd's *Margaret,* 1845; to Edward Bellamy's *Looking Backward,* 1888; and to Henry Olerich's *A Cityless and a Countryless World,* 1893); and, on the other, to the activities of Josiah Warren and Etienne Cabet, of John Noyes and Joseph Smith, Saint-Simon and Enfantin, Fourier and Owen. Broadacres is the latest and probably the last of a series of cooperative community projects that proliferated in the mid nineteenth century—especially in the United States, where at least a hundred and seventy-eight were actually launched.[41]

39. *Ibid.,* p. 244.
40. *Ibid.,* p. 245.
41. Cf. Edmund Wilson, *To the Finland Station* (New York: Doubleday & Company, Inc., 1947), p. 103; Arthur E. Bestor, Jr., *Backwoods Utopias* (Philadelphia: University of Pennsylvania Press, 1950); Louis Vernon Parrington, *American Dreams* (Providence, R. I., Brown University Studies, 1947).

Although its roots were old and deep, the communitarian movement as such was coetaneous with Romanticism, being marked from beginning to end by the enthusiastic embracing of polar extremes that was characteristic of the Romantic outlook. It originated in the 1790s, as did Broadacre City in the 1930s, in response to social upheaval and distress. One of its first manifestations in the mainstream of cultural happenings (as against a variety of marginal prefigurations) is to be found in the Pantisocracy scheme which was pressed forward in 1793 and for a year or two thereafter by Coleridge and Southey (both of whom were Unitarians like Wright).

I . . . formed a plan [wrote Coleridge] as harmless as it was extravagant, of trying the experiment of human perfectibility on the banks of the Susquehannah; where our little society, in its second generation, was to have combined the innocence of the Patriarchal Age with the knowledge and general refinements of European culture; and where I dreamed that in the sober evening of my life I should behold the cottages of independence in the undivided dale of industry.[42]

Pastoral simplicity and cultural refinement, residential separation and industrial union: here is Wright's formula, set forth already a hundred and forty years before the publication of his own plan!

In the first years of the depression Wright was in close touch with the sorely tried farmers and villagers of southern Wisconsin, but at the same time he was wholly out of touch with the world of political and economic affairs. His position was precisely that of the nineteenth-century communitarians. "None of these political idealists," says Edmund Wilson, "understood the real mechanics of social change nor could they foresee the inevitable development of the system which they so much destested. They could only devise imaginary systems as antithetical to the real one as possible and attempt to construct models of these, assuming that the example would be contagious." [43] This was literally the nature of Wright's activity: instead of engaging in political action that might have affected public policy at some level, he and his apprentices spent long hours in the mid-thirties constructing a large

42. From the eleventh issue of *The Friend.* Quoted in Fairchild, *The Romantic Quest.*

43. Edmund Wilson, *To the Finland Station,* p. 102.

model of Broadacres that was later exhibited at various places, presumably in the quite vain expectation that its example would be contagious.

Characteristic of virtually all the communitarian ventures is an odd mixture of radical equalitarianism and autocracy. Although each community was designed to insure the rights and liberties of its members, its governing idea or program is usually found to have been the invention of a single, quasi-prophetic, often eccentric leader, and its only chance of survival lay in his being able to maintain, as did Owen at New Lanark and Noyes at Oneida, a benevolently despotic control over all its affairs. Wright foresaw this necessity, as had Rousseau in defining the role of the Legislator in *The Social Contract*: in Broadacre City "the agent of the state in all matters of land allotment or improvement, or in matters affecting the harmony of the whole, is the architect."[44] In other words, the entire life of Broadacres would have come under his jurisdiction, for what is there that does not affect the harmony of the whole? Wright's confidence in the architect is partly a matter of egoism, partly an expression of a Veblenesque and characteristically American faith in the skill of the engineer, whose training and intelligence are presumed to raise him above petty partisanship and human frailty. Still more important, I believe, is the connection between Wright's governing architect and the Old Testament image of the king. For at the center of ancient Israel there stands not a legalistic constitution but a *man*—not a theory of government but a *person*. Wright could have accepted nothing less.

At bottom Wright's concern was not with economic and social problems, either in our present society or in his imaginary one, but with the nature of the "free pattern" which Broadacres was to exemplify. That pattern possesses something of the continuity of a growing tree, something of the discontinuity of a *family* tree; it is composed, not as buildings or cities have traditionally been composed, but in the manner of a landscape painting. For nothing is more important to it than the perspective experience of the indwelling observer-member who knows himself to be comprehended, even as the member of a family knows himself to belong, within a pattern that allows him freely to

44. "Broadacre City: A New Community Plan," p. 246.

grow and to become fully himself. The basic social unit is the family, which contains the nuclear principle that governs the entire community.

That this was the central principle of American communitarianism had been recognized clearly enough by one of its leading prophets, John Humphrey Noyes. Discussing Owenism and Fourierism in 1870, he said:

> We must not think of the two great socialistic revivals as altogether heterogeneous and separate. Their partizans maintained theoretical opposition to each other; but after all the main idea of both was the enlargement of the home—*the extension of family union beyond the little man-and-wife circle to large corporations.* In this the two movements were one; and this was the charming idea that caught the attention and stirred the enthusiasm of the American people.[45]

In the 1830s and '40s the idea plainly had the power to stir thousands of Americans to unwarrantedly enthusiastic action. In the 1930s it had it no longer.

What shall we say, then, of Wright's proposal? Was it wholly idle and useless? One's assessment must depend, of course, upon one's point of view. To the practical politician and the ordinary citizen Broadacres has meant less than nothing. Judged by the pragmatic standards of the workaday world, it is so irrelevant that it has simply been ignored—for the realization of Broadacre City (which must be "everywhere or nowhere") would require the abrogation of the Constitution of the United States, the elimination of thousands of governmental bodies from the make-up of the state, the confiscation of all lands by right of eminent domain but without compensation, the demolition of all cities and therewith the obliteration of every evidence of the country's history, the rehousing of the entire population, the retraining of millions of persons so as to enable them to be self-sustaining farmers, and other difficulties too numerous to mention. As a practicable program it does not even deserve discussion.

Today that may seem self-evident. Thirty-five years ago, however, when Marxian analysis was at the height of its popularity among Amer-

45. John Humphrey Noyes, *History of American Socialisms* (Philadelphia, 1870), quoted in Bestor's *Backwoods Utopias,* p. 54.

ican intellectuals, the plan could be taken very seriously indeed. Shortly after its publication it was subjected to lacerating criticism by Meyer Schapiro,[46] but not for the reasons mentioned above; Schapiro was offended, instead, by the inadequacy of Wright's economic analysis, by his indifference toward even the existence of social classes, to say nothing of their disparate interests and mutual antagonisms, by his reactionary and regressive (if not fascist) vision of a static social order, frozen at a pitifully low level of productivity, and so on. Although Schapiro's arraignment of the plan is sound enough and has lately been seconded by David Riesman, it seems much less trenchant today than it did in 1938. We can see more clearly now that Broadacres and Marxism are sprung from the same root, and that Schapiro's attack on Wright was inspired in some degree with that special vehemence which the righteous reserve for the denunciation of heresy. In our present time of disenchantment the significant issues must be sought elsewhere.

In *The Living City,* the architect introduced among the illustrative drawings, but did not identify by name, many of the buildings he had designed over a period of some fifty years: there is the first project for the Willey house, the Pew house, the Steel Cathedral, the Price Tower, the Lake Tahoe barges, the new Dallas theater, a latterday version of the Quadruple Block, and so on. Although the form of the City's small industrial plants is not specified in detail, the Johnson building would probably serve as their general prototype. Since the Steel Cathedral is included, it seems likely that even the Mile High Illinois would somewhere find its place in the over-all plan. Wright's introduction of these various projects should not, I think, be attributed to expediency or to a thrifty desire on his part to make further use of existing material—though he was given to doing exactly this in putting together his frequently repetitious books. What he wanted to make clear, I believe, is that there is an underlying principle that establishes the unity of his life's work, and that that principle is best expressed in Broadacre City. To judge Broadacres is to judge everything he created —and vice versa. We must try to discover and to assess that general principle.

46. Meyer Schapiro, "Architect's Utopia," *Partisan Review,* IV (March 1938), 43.

SEVEN
ASSESSMENT

IT HAS BEEN MY CONTENTION, FIRST OF ALL, THAT Wright was, in keeping with the oldest and best traditions of architectural art, conservative—that he understood that the art of building has generally had as its chief goal the clarification and stabilization of the city, or of the body politic, by providing the community with enduring symbols of those modes of relatedness that make possible a meaningful and coherent social order. One of his principal claims to distinction lies in this: that he kept alive a rich and poetic conception of architectural metaphor at a time when the theory of architecture was being reduced on every hand to a matter of petty problem-solving and of desiccated technics.

The New Eden and the New Jerusalem

I have argued at some length that the key to Wright's thought, and perhaps to Romanticism in general, is to be found in a characteristically Biblical and anti-Hellenic emphasis on the dynamics of personal being, as against the static and objective being-of-things; that that emphasis tended to express itself in terms of polar tensions; and that the polarities with which Wright struggled from the beginning, both in his life and in his architecture, are fully exemplified in the Kaufmann house and the Johnson building. One can characterize the opposition in many ways—the open against the closed, the private against the public, multiplicity against unity, the centrifugal against the centripetal, Nature against the City, freedom against loyalty, anarchy against panarchy—but consistently I find two poles toward which Wright was simultaneously attracted.

Moreover, I have pointed to a number of relationships between him and Rousseau. There are grounds for drawing a comparison, I believe, between Wright's act, in 1936, of putting up those opposite buildings and Rousseau's, in 1762, of publishing at the same time *Emile* and its opposite number, *The Social Contract*. Each pair of works may well be considered to mark the culmination of its author's career, and each consists of a moving plea for the freedom of the individual in Nature, matched by an equally ardent declaration in favor of collectivity and agreement within an organized society. In *Emile* Rousseau speaks out against institutions, laws, governments, habits, traditional education—against all those things which ordinarily make possible the binding together of a lasting social order; while in *The Social Contract* his principal concern is with the General Will and with securing the total submission of the individual to the Sovereign, or to the political power that belongs to the society as a whole. In *Emile,* as in Fallingwater, the idea of Nature is all-important; in *The Social Contract,* as in the Johnson building, it is absent and irrelevant—for Rousseau explicitly declares that the act of civil association is a matter of convention, not of Nature. *Emile* is essentially anti-urban in tone, inveighing against the destructive effects of city life; while *The Social Contract* is devoted exclusively to the problem of designing a city.

Yet I do not in the least mean to suggest that these polarities were invented by Rousseau, or that they were in any way restricted to the style-period of Romanticism. As Wright well knew, they come down to us from an ethical and religious tradition of immense antiquity, the history of which can be traced back at least to the sixth century B.C. in both the East and West; but the path by which they entered the main current of European thought is by way of the Bible and Christianity.

We have had occasion already to mention the prophetic aspects of Wright's thought and to discuss its ultimate derivation from the ancient patterns of Hebrew expression. He himself spoke of Jesus as the very embodiment of the ideal to which he was devoted, even though he had no regard whatever for the Christianity of the organized churches. Nor had Rousseau, though his contempt for institutionalized religion did not prevent him from declaring, as we have seen, his love for the Gospel and his veneration of Jesus Christ.

No doubt both Wright and Rousseau found many things in the Gospel that appealed to them, but perhaps for both men the crux of the matter lay in two statements, or kinds of statement, one finds in the sayings of Jesus. The first has to do with the primacy of the individual: "The kingdom of God cometh not with observation . . . for behold, the kingdom of God is within you" (Luke 17:20-21). Here is the basis of that strain of idealism that is proclaimed in Emerson's injunction, "Speak your latent conviction and it shall be the universal sense." Like Rousseau, but unlike Marx and his followers, Wright was never given to making meticulous observations and careful analyses of the concrete facts of our socio-historical situation; he staked everything, instead, upon the validity of his "latent conviction" and prophesied on the strength of his personal inspiration, as did Isaiah and Jeremiah.

And secondly, there is the extraordinary ideal of relatedness which Jesus expounded: "Verily I say unto you, Whatsoever ye shall bind on earth shall be bound in heaven; and whatsoever ye shall loose on earth shall be loosed in heaven" (Matt. 18:18). For Plato, as we noted earlier, goodness pertained to binding only, and evil to loosing only. For Jesus, however, loosing is as important as binding, freeing as important as uniting. It is not hard to discover what it was he wanted to loosen: it was the bonds of legal and legalistic relatedness which were imposed by the established institutions of society. One thinks immediately of his many strictures on religious traditionalism and even on ordinary family loyalty. "And everyone that hath forsaken houses, or brethren, or sisters, or father, or mother, or wife, or children, or lands, for my name's sake, shall receive an hundredfold, and shall inherit everlasting life" (Matt. 19:29). "Think not that I am come to send peace on earth: I came not to send peace, but a sword. For I am come to set a man at variance against his father, and the daughter against her mother, and the daughter-in-law against her mother-in-law. *And a man's foes shall be they of his own household*" (Matt. 10:34-36).

In place of the ancient modes of obligatory relationship Jesus would institute a new binding, based upon the voluntary participation of small groups of free persons. "Again I say unto you, that if two of you shall agree on earth as touching anything that they shall ask, it shall be done for them of my Father which is in heaven. For where two or three are gathered together in my name, there am I in the midst of them" (Matt. 18:19-20). It was this conception of voluntary brotherhood that united the apostolic church, gave rise to the early monasteries, sustained the lay confraternities of the Middle Ages, and inspired the founders of innumerable pietistic groups before and after the Reformation; and it is this same ideal which underlies Tennyson's notion of the Round Table—and Wright's of the Taliesin Fellowship.

Christian art abounds in images in which the polar extremes of joining and of loosing are represented. Let us juxtapose, for instance, Piero's Brera altarpiece and Bellini's "Stigmatization of St. Francis" at the Frick—two north-Italian works that are separated in date by less than ten years. Each represents the highest and most perfect fulfillment of one aspect of the Christian ideal. In a context of windowless "total architecture" Piero celebrates the virtues of membership, of unqualified involvement within a closed and eternally stable society, of submission to the regulatory discipline of the Sovereign. The six saints who form the Virgin's court can be identified by name, but they could be replaced by any other six one might care to select. St. Francis appears here wholly as member, his position being interchangeable with that of any other citizen of the celestial kingdom. Bellini, on the other hand, celebrates the utterly unique and intensely personal religious experience—a moment of agonizing poignancy that comes to the saint when he is alone in the midst of nature. A Wordsworth or a Thoreau could have added nothing whatever to Bellini's presentation of that experience, in which the smallest leaf and pebble are shown to be "apparelled in celestial light." Piero places his figures in a palace, therefore at the heart of the city and at the seat of government, while Bellini states explicitly, as other painters of the subject generally had not done, that St. Francis received his transfiguring vision outside and away from the city.

PLATE XXVIII

PLATE XXX

In order to understand the implications of all this for Wright's architecture, we must go one step further and consider the two images of paradise which have persisted side by side in Christian thought: heaven as a garden and heaven as a strong city—the New Eden and the New Jerusalem. In the one is pictured the heavenly loosing, in the other the heavenly binding. The garden represents ultimate blessedness as the enjoyment of perfect freedom in a setting of unlimited horizontal expanse and of the most varied and sensuous delights; while the city declares it to be one of perfect mutuality—of membership and security within an enclosed setting of steadfast order.

This is the framework within which Wright made his prophetic avowals. At the one pole stands the intimate private family, a handful of persons whose relationship to one another is marked by spontaneous delight: it is natural, growing, changing, dynamic, free—as open and as variable as the landscape itself. The nature in the midst of which the family dwells is no mere composite of biological phenomena; it is Isaiah's nature, in which the very hills may break forth into singing and the trees of the field clap their hands. The family's house lies far from

PLATE XXXI

the city and deep in the woodlands that are held to be, in essence, a paradisiacal garden. At the opposite pole (but comprising, ideally, the same persons) stands the voluntary group, working together in a common cause in the midst of the city, which is itself identified with the binding functions of civilization and a common culture. Its building is closed and fortress-like, showing forth the nature of the city as "ein feste Burg." The city, too, is Isaiah's: "Look upon Zion, the city of our solemnities: thine eyes shall see Jersusalem a quiet habitation, a tabernacle that shall not be taken down; not one of the stakes thereof shall be removed, neither shall any of the cords thereof be broken" (Isaiah 33:20).

PLATE XXIX

The Pertinency of Polarity

BUT EVEN if we grant all this, what is its relevance to twentieth-century America? What conceivable value or significance has it for a world that is not especially Christian and has no interest at all in visions of paradise? If we judge significance by popularity, or acceptability, or immediate utility for problem-solving, then perhaps it has very little. Nevertheless, there are at least two things that need to be said in defense of Wright's position. The first has to do with the general principle of polarity; the second, with the historical tradition that Wright represents.

While I am not perfectly sure that I know what St. Paul meant when he declared that he knew that "all things work together for good," I presume that he was pointing to the fact that goodness is a relative concept, involving a polarity between the good and its opposite or privative. It is the function of evil, he might have said, to make goodness possible; for if there were no evil, the ethical dimension of our being would be obliterated. Certainly it has been a common failing of utopian thought to leave out of account this interdependence. As Warner Wick observes, "Intellectual balance relegates a belief in the inevitability of a classless social paradise to the realm of pseudo-theology, for the concept of a good without its correlative is a rational scandal." [1] By contrast, much of the vigor of Reformation thought may

1. Warner A. Wick, *Metaphysics and the New Logic* (Chicago: University of Chicago Press, 1942), p. 108.

be attributed to its almost Manichaean insistence upon the power of Satan, without which the goodness of God could not be realized.

This Christian insight is nowhere more clearly expressed than in the paintings of Rembrandt, who was perennially drawn to those themes, such as "The Return of the Prodigal Son," "The Reconciliation of David and Absalom," and "The Good Samaritan," in which goodness has been reached by way of evil. Darkness for Rembrandt is the correlative of light—a relationship that was denied by the Impressionists, who rejected along with it the moral and spiritual tensions of Biblical thought. Yet it does not follow that Rembrandt's darks are simply negative and a symbol of evil. As we can see in his sunset landscapes (and virtually all his landscapes are of sunset or twilight scenes), Rembrandt found goodness in the night as well as in the day, in rest as well as in labor, in relaxation as well as in tension, in ending as well as in beginning, in "sweet death" as well as in life. Whatever serves as the correlative of the good participates in that goodness, whether it be pleasant or painful. As Wright himself expressed it, "In the last analysis there is no evil because shadow itself is of the light." Here he perhaps goes too far, for in denying the reality of evil and in averring that shadow is itself a phenomenon of light, he comes perilously close to embracing the hedonistic and quasi-Impressionist experientialism toward which he was always attracted, despite his desire to hold fast to a more demanding ethical tradition. Nevertheless, in sensing that evil "works for good" Wright reveals his commitment to a fundamental principle of Biblical thought.

So it is with the two images of paradise, Eden and Zion: each is the other's *contrapletion,* to use John W. Buckham's term for describing the complementary relationship of polarity. For the full realization of blessedness both must be present, Zion in the midst of Eden, even as we see them in the Van Eycks' "Adoration of the Mystic Lamb." Neither city nor garden is sufficient of itself.

Herein lies the great merit of Broadacre City, which should not be looked upon as a practicable plan for social action but as a declaration of ultimate principle. Recently we have seen our architects tumbling over one another in their eagerness to follow Mies in housing anything and everything—private family, school, whiskey company, law court—in monotonously similar glass-walled boxes, thereby urging upon us an ideal of geometrical purity and of austere intelligence that stands against the "chaos" of modern life, the reality of which is presumed to be evident for all to see in the blighted appearance of our cities. The presence of a Lever House or a Time & Life Building amidst the cluttered heterogeneity of a modern city may seem to hold out to us the promise of a social order that will be sunlit, clean, efficient, and somehow beyond the reach of dilapidation and decay. The promise owes its attractiveness mainly to the visible contrast between the new precision and the old confusion, the new glitter and the old drabness; but whether a timeless new city of steel and glass would in truth afford us a satisfying frame of reference for human existence is debatable, to say the least. The goodness of efficiency and of all-governing intelligence might well turn out to have no genuine correlative, and therefore to be something other than goodness, if the new architecture were actually to supplant the old which for the time being sustains it.

Now Wright's architecture also stands against the tawdriness and banality of the world, against mundane convention and empty pretentiousness, and claims to bear witness to a new birth of cultivated civilization. Alone among modern architects, however, Wright could have declared that even if every building in the nation were replaced and its architecture were Wrightian from coast to coast, still the goodness espoused in every design would be evident—in fact, only then fully evident—since for every kind of structure there would exist an opposite and correlative kind, even as the Kaufmann house is the correlative of the Johnson building.

Surely it is well that we should be reminded that man is an ethical being who is not only capable of envisioning paradise but is compelled to do so in order to know the shape and residence of goodness. Without that vision one may all too easily mistake efficiency or economy or aesthetic homogeneity or "structural honesty" or convenience or some other small and conditional virtue for an ideal of ultimate significance, as the contemporary architect and designer have often done; or else one may be forced to avow the utter meaninglessness of our experience, as some kinds of modern painter have had to do. Broadacres, on the other hand, affirms the necessity of our upholding an interpretation of man and the world which has been handed down through some hundred generations—an interpretation to which the polarity of Eden and Zion is an essential key.

This brings me to my second point, which has to do with the relation of Wright's architecture to a historical tradition in which the Biblical idea of paradise plays a significant part. When Wright insisted that he wanted to create an *American* architecture, he did not in the least mean a style that would "express" the culture or civilization of the United States. On the contrary, he never ceased to denounce the "pseudo-civilization" of our Usonian "mobocracy" as barbarous, degenerate, servile, and wholly lacking in anything that might conceivably be called a genuine culture. No, the America he had in mind lies both in the past and in the future. It is bound up with an idea that takes us back to the very beginnings of what was long called the New World (the very name is millennialistic)—a world that seemed then to hold a promise of salvation for those who could free themselves from an effete and degraded Old World.

After beholding the tropical beauty of the Caribbean islands and the grace of their naked inhabitants, Columbus himself came to believe that his third voyage had brought him close to the edge of the Garden of Eden, which probably lay, he surmised, in the vicinity of the modern country of Brazil. Amerigo Vespucci, though having reservations about the excellence of primitive man and his society, yet could write:

> They have no cloth, either of wool, flax, or cotton, because they have no need of it; nor have they any private property, everything being held in common. They live amongst themselves without a king or ruler, each man being his own master, and having as many wives as they please. . . . They have no temples and no laws, nor are they idolators. What more can I say! They live according to nature. . . .[2]

Amerigo discovered what he had been prepared to discover by the two-thousand-year-old tradition of Judeo-Christian prophecy: he believed that he had found unfallen man, living outside history and in perfect harmony with the rest of creation, enjoying simultaneously both total communality and absolute personal freedom, Zion in the midst of Eden.

2. Charles L. Sanford, *The Quest for Paradise* (Urbana: University of Illinois Press, 1961), p. 57.

Yet the notion of either discovering or achieving an earthly paradise is relatively remote from the thinking of Biblical and early Christian writers. Though the Christians of the apostolic church may have looked forward impatiently to the Second Coming, they were not preoccupied with, or optimistic about, the historical future of earthly society. It is with Joachim of Floris (c. 1135-1202) that we first encounter in Christian thinking the idea that history itself is going to be fulfilled in a new Golden Age of earthly bliss. Joachim maintained, in fact, that the third and final period of history, the Age of the Holy Spirit, had already been initiated by St. Benedict, and that at its culmination, when Elijah would reappear on earth, there would be established a universal society, to be characterized (like Broadacres) by the frugal simplicity and perfect communality of the monastic life at its best. Following in the wake of Joachim, the German mystic Heinrich Suso could declare, in 1330, "I belong to the Liberty of Nature, and all that my nature desires I satisfy. . . . I am a natural man." [3] Frank Lloyd Wright might well have made the same avowal. The natural man for whom he designed the Natural House is inconceivable apart from the myth of Adam, the essential man who was indeed created to experience the Liberty of Nature.

The discovery of the New World and the early reports of explorers such as Amerigo stirred up a wave of interest in the perfectibility of human society. An immediate consequence, of course, was the writing of More's *Utopia*. It seems likely, too, that Bosch's *Millennium* (if we may take Wilhelm Fraenger's interpretation of the so-called "Garden of Earthly Delights" to be within hailing distance of the truth), what with its vision of hundreds of naked men and women disporting themselves innocently in a garden full of marvels, was partly inspired by such reports. Bosch's Adamitism, if such it was, prefigures the attitudes toward "free love" with which Wright was so deeply concerned around 1912.

In his recent book, *The Quest for Paradise*, Charles L. Sanford has demonstrated how important was this Joachitic eschatology to the discoverers and early settlers of the New World, how continuously strong has been the expectation, among Americans, of witnessing the

3. *Ibid.*, p.13.

establishment of the kingdom of God on earth, and how that faith is still sufficiently powerful to shape the foreign policy of the United States. Perhaps it is one of the merits of the Broadacres plan that it compels us to contemplate anew that vision of an agrarian paradise which filled the dreams of so many of the settlers of this country, which was still taken seriously by men of the time and caliber of Franklin and Jefferson, and which we may hope, at least, is an indestructible element in the mythology of the American nation. "Give me your tired, your poor, your huddled masses yearning to breathe free. . . ." This, too, is the language of prophecy—"Come unto me all ye who are heavy laden"—but more in the manner of Joachim of Floris than of the Bible.

The Central Self

SPEAKING OF an idea that is widely encountered among primitive peoples of the kind Europeans had seriously to be concerned with only after the time of Columbus, Mircea Eliade says: "Every microcosm, every inhabited region, has what may be called a 'Centre'; that is to say, a place that is sacred above all. It is there, in that Centre, that the sacred manifests itself in its totality." [4] It troubles some persons in our society (cf. Hans Sedylmayr's *Verlust der Mitte*) that we have no such center—no sacred places, no destinations for pilgrimage of the sort that have so often been marked out by great buildings in past ages. Our architects have seemed almost obsessed with the idea of center and have peppered the landscape with community centers, shopping centers, medical centers, civic centers, information centers, cultural centers, research centers, computer centers, and so on; but not one of these possesses the kind of religio-political significance that can inspire and sustain great architecture. As genuine Centers they are trivial.

In fact, since about the year 1500, architects have found it increasingly difficult to produce buildings that could be said to possess the kind of centrality that so obviously inheres in the great pilgrimage and cathedral churches of the Middle Ages, and is just as obviously

4. Mircea Eliade, *Images and Symbols,* trans. P. Mairet (London: Harvill Press, 1961), p. 39.

lacking from the architecture of the nineteenth-century revivals. Though it is not easy to say why this is the case, it would appear that the architect's deepening difficulties can be correlated with the rise of portraiture and landscape painting. It can probably be set forth as a general principle that in a society that posits the existence of a Cosmic Tree or Primaeval Mountain at the center of the universe there will be no landscape art; for where landscape is a matter of concern, the Center has been shifted from some external object to within the self. The self has become self-centered.

This is the sense of Jesus' statement, "The kingdom of God is within you." In his forty-first letter to Lucilius, Seneca, a contemporary of Jesus, made a similar assertion: "God is near you, he is with you, he is within you." Seneca goes on, then, to cite two specific instances of his intimate intuition of the presence of deity, both of which are *landscape* experiences of the solitary person in a remote natural setting. "A true man belongs to no other time and place," wrote Emerson, "but in the center of things. Where he is, there is nature." One could not express more succinctly the sustaining conviction of the landscapist. Wright's architecture was conceived in defense of that conviction, which has been abandoned by the majority of twentieth-century artists in favor of an attitude toward the self in which neither the religio-mythical element of centrality nor the link with nature is preserved.

If the center lies within the self, then the self must reject any claim to centrality that may be made by the state and its institutions. Significantly, it was the landscapist Peter Brueghel who, in his "Tower of Babel" paintings, mocked the pretensions of Madrid and of Rome, just when the Escorial was being laid out and when the unfinished Church of St. Peter towered like some mammoth Roman ruin on Vatican Hill. The paintings are superb landscapes in which architecture figures only as a monstrous and absurd intruder. Concomitantly, Brueghel avowed his own preference for the unpretentious life of the farmer. In his little "Adoration of the Magi in the Snow" (1567) he shows the birth of Jesus to take place in a peasant village in which the great stone chateau of some extinct dynasty of lords is falling into ruin.

One can easily see that Wright dispersed Broadacre City over the face of the earth in order to free persons from the destructive effects of the megalopolis; but perhaps a second look is required to perceive that the ultimate importance of Broadacres lay in the fact that it was sprung from the wholly personal center of Wright's own mind. "We want men and women who shall renovate life and our social state," wrote Emerson—persons who were as convinced as he that "nothing is at last sacred but the integrity of your own mind." Finding himself at the center of nature, the landscapist (at least until the advent of Impressionism) discovered, as did Emerson, that his existence was of central importance in an ethical sense, also. Jesus did not say simply that "God is within you," but that "The *Kingdom* of God is within you." The concept of *Regnum Dei* implies that by virtue of being central, the individual is also responsible, even *absolutely* responsible.

It may seem gratuitous and presumptuous that Wright should have assumed responsibility for revising every aspect of the life of the American nation—but then in fact he did not, since, as we have already noted, he never engaged in political action. Broadacres is mainly an assertion about the self—about Wright's own self and, in general, about a kind of sacred and central selfhood that he believed is being obliterated in the present-day world. If we take the currently popular *avant-garde* art to be a reliable indicator, then surely that is the case; for both landscape and portraiture have virtually disappeared from modern art. On the other hand, the overwhelming majority of living Americans detest that art and are in some measure devoted to those older ideas that are reflected in kinds of painting that go back to the seventeenth century and before. If nothing else, Broadacres is a conservative appeal in defense of an idea of selfhood that is grievously threatened in this day of the "market personality" and the "other-directed man."

Wright and the State

YET ONE may make certain objections which are not easily put aside.

In 1908 Wright said of his architecture, "At no point does it involve denial of the elemental law and order inherent in all great architecture: rather, it is a declaration of love for the spirit of that law and order." But of exactly what law and order? Surely nothing is more important to the maintenance of any society than its conception of law and of lawfulness, nor is anything more clearly evident than that the conception undergirding the American state is Greco-Roman rather than Hebraic in nature. The state is based upon the idea of the "mixed constitution," as we have received it from Polybius and Cicero, in which a prudent balance is struck among autocratic, representative, and democratic factors in the administration of public affairs. The authors of the Constitution reveal themselves to have been heirs, as well, to the Renaissance tradition of civic and republican Humanism. Central to that whole tradition is the idea of the vote—a quantitative or quantificatory political device that is utterly foreign to Biblical and romantic thought. It presupposes the ultimate significance and validity of adding, or of mathematical determination, no less than does the ordering of the Parthenon and of Plato's ideal state.

For a century and a half after the founding of the government of the United States it was the common practice to house its public agencies and institutions in ordered and columniated buildings that were descended, in one way or another, from Greek and Roman prototypes. Ever since the beginning of the Modern Movement in architecture, we have been urged to believe that all such latter-day classicism was merely a matter of imitative revivalism, therefore fundamentally inappropriate to our modern world. But was it, in fact? Have we in any sense outgrown or passed beyond that ancient faith in the principle that citizens must be regarded as equal and equally responsible members? It seems curious and disturbing that, in the midst of the social upheaval that is now taking place in the United States, the notion that "all men are created equal" is everywhere proclaimed, yet neither our artists nor our architects are willing or able to produce a visual affirmation in defense of the religio-philosophical tradition from which the notion is derived and apart from which it may well be regarded as meaningless verbiage. For there is assuredly no scientific or "objective" basis for believing that men are equal. One must consider the possibility, at least, that the modern architect's efforts at reshaping both the visual appearance and the philosophical basis of the city's structure are presumptuous in the extreme and an uncalled-for negation of what the populace still, for the most part, cherishes. In view of the appalling destruction which political violence has already brought about in the twentieth century, to say nothing of what the future may hold, we may have cause to wonder if the architect might not best serve us by reasserting, as architects have generally done in ages past, the validity of the historic bases of agreement and of social order.

In the years before and after the Second World War, Wright's admirers sometimes lamented the fact that, despite the enormous increase in the number of governmental buildings in the country, he had never been awarded a commission by any governmental body, national, state, or local. Looking back upon the matter now, we can see that there was perhaps a certain justification for that indifference or refusal, since Wright's architecture was fundamentally opposed to the Greco-Roman foundations of the American state. The extent to which this is the case can most clearly be seen in the design for a new Arizona State Capitol that Wright gratuitously put forward in the 1950s, in protest against the state's having accepted an uncommonly dull design of block-like Miesian simplicity.[5] What he proposed was a conspicuously Wrightian fantasy, of which the largest element was to be a huge hexagonal greenhouse of a room, roofed over with a pyramidal structure composed of small hexagons, that was to be called the Arizona Hall. Here the history of the state was to be "memorialized."

All buildings stand, of course, in a certain relation to both past and future. Once a building has been completed, in no matter what style, it belongs to the past. On the other hand, every building is erected in the expectation that it will endure into an indefinite future and will continue to affect men's thoughts and behaviour in more or less definable ways for a period of time that is almost always assumed to be longer than the lifetime of its architect and its builders. More than any other kind of symbolic artifact, buildings have the power to declare that some pattern of relationships has been established, has been made to stand (whence the word "state"—from the past participle of the verb *stare,* to stand), and they are able to project that pattern into the future of an on-going human community. Nowhere is that capacity more important than in *state* buildings, for, generally speaking, the endurance of lesser institutions depends upon the state's steadfastness. For ages past it has been the common practice of the builders of civic buildings to represent (or, by means of stylistic associations, to allude to) certain modes of relatedness that may be taken to constitute

5. For a discussion of this project from another point of view, see my article, "Frank Lloyd Wright and the Problem of Historical Perspective," *Journal of the Society of Architectural Historians,* Vol. XXVI, No. 4 (December 1967), pp. 234-37.

the established "frame of reference" within which the leaders of the state may formulate laws and issue directives with regard to the proximate future. Though the past itself may be as immutable as the pyramids, the legislator's *conception* of the past, or of what mainly matters in our inheritance, is mutable—is subject to being shaped at least in some measure by the imagery of architecture.

In all the state capitols and civic buildings that were erected in the United States prior to the advent of the Modern Movement, this basic relationship between past and future was maintained. Each building made visible men's acceptance of a tradition, even as it avowed the necessity of modifying that same tradition in the light of altered circumstances. The building served as a landmark in time as well as in space, upholding an order of things that was taken to constitute the *ethos* of the *ethnos* (or community of men) that had inhabited a given *ethos* (or accustomed abode) over an extended period. Apart from men's continued acceptance of that *ethos,* ethical government is manifestly impossible—as the recent history of the American presidency has demonstrated.

Now Wright understood all this better than has any other modern builder. "This abstraction we are calling Civilization—how was it made and how is it misused or being lost now? By 'abstraction' I mean taking the essence of a thing—anything—*the pattern of it,* as the substance of reality. Incidental effects aside, the *heart* of the matter would lie in the abstraction if well made. . . . Our customs, costumes, habits, habitations, and manners, all are, or should be, such abstractions; and made, as such, true to the great abstraction we call civilization. . . . Once made, although the ritual may become 'obsolete,' the original abstraction will be cherished by man . . ." [6] One could hardly justify with greater cogency the motivations of Thomas Jefferson, whom Wright greatly admired, in building Monticello, the University of Virginia, and the Virginia State Capitol in classic style.

And yet when Wright undertook to design a capitol for Phoenix, he proceeded on a different basis altogether. One might say that he chose to reverse the relation of architecture to past and future. His

6. Frank Lloyd Wright, *A Testament* (New York: Horizon Press, 1957), p. 58.

design is wholly unrelated to any of the "cherished abstractions" that have lain at the heart of what it is we have inherited in the way of civilization. The static structure of the building as such refers, if to anything at all, to a quasi-millenary future that is sprung entirely from Wright's own mind: while what is centrally housed inside the building is not the future-oriented functioning of state government but a memorialization of the past-as-process. Rather than reminding governmental officials of the abiding *ethos,* it exhibits the state's history to the citizen-as-tourist or citizen-as-spectator . . . though just what there was about that history that would have been worthy of being so exhibited, and just how, Wright would probably have found it hard to specify. Since the building itself disavows any relationship whatever to the history and wholeness of the city of Phoenix, one can scarcely imagine its existing within the confines of that city. Like so much of Wright's *oeuvre,* it belongs to Broadacre City, where there will be neither past nor future, nor any need for anyone to pattern his life after the "customs, costumes, habits, habitations, and manners" of his ancestors.

Perhaps Wright came finally to understand something of this limitation or shortcoming in his architectural thought, for he proceeded along altogether different lines when, at the very end of his long career, he was at last given a civic commission—that of building the Marin County Civic Center in San Rafael, California. It is interesting to see what he chose to do. Without entirely abandoning the characteristic shapes and rhythms of his own style, he managed to produce an extraordinarily *Roman* building: a long, low, ground-hugging, arcuated structure that lies between and among low hills as if it were a section of a Roman aqueduct. Yet its many arches (large, middle-sized, and small, as in the Pont du Gard) are not the door-like, figure-framing shapes that the Romans preferred; they are low, rippling, segmental arches that call to mind at once a long tradition of bridge building that extends from Telford through Captain Eads to Maillart. Though Wright would have had no taste for Roman conceptions of empire, there is one Roman idea he would probably have liked very much indeed—namely, the designation of the chief religious official of the state, and later the emperor, as *pontifex maximus* or, literally, as "head bridge builder." It would not be inappropriate to use the same title for the Architect in Broadacre City, whose function is would be to design the over-all network of roads and interchanges and also to maintain "bridges" of communication among the citizens, seeing to it that nothing should be allowed to disrupt "the harmony of the whole."

Even so, the Civic Center is first and foremost a Wrightian invention, attesting to the uniqueness of its architect's talent but having little connection with those traditional patterns that he knew men should cherish, whether or not their aboriginal "rituals" might have become "obsolete." To the very end, he was unable to accept those traditions as binding upon himself—as making any claim upon him that might cause him to place obedient emulation ahead of personal originality, membership ahead of individuality. For all his Whitmanesque enthusiasm about the promise of the American people, he could not give significant weight to the role of citizen or to the concept of citizenship; for to have done so would have deprived him of his distinctive standpoint, which was that of the hortatory prophet . . . and for obvious reasons it is not the role of either an Isaiah or a Jeremiah to build temples and capitols and courthouses.

To the end, the nuclear occasions for Wright were to be found in the life of the family and in the productive activity of fellow-workers in voluntary association with one another. For all his misgivings about the sufficiency of the suburb, as he had come to understand it in Oak Park, he remains in the minds of most of us an essentially suburban architect, caught in the polarity not so much of Nature and the City as of the Suburb and the Factory. The grievous limitations of that peculiarly American polarity have been poignantly detailed by Eugen Rosenstock-Huessy: in the suburb there is achieved an artificial tranquility and geniality by the deliberate elimination, insofar as possible, of traumatic experiences of birth and death, conflict and contrast; while in the factory there prevails an efficient anonymity, an anonymous efficiency, that deprives most workers of any sense of responsible identity, of any occasion for being *persons* in a full sense of the word.[7] Indeed, one may protest that Wright did not address himself adequately to even that polarity: especially in his later years he attracted commissions that placed his houses farther and farther out into the countryside, where

7. Eugen Rosenstock-Huessy, *The Christian Future* (New York: Charles Scribner's Sons, 1946), pp. 12-29.

problems of communal agreement could be largely ignored (even though it was during those same years that the American suburb was mushrooming at an appalling rate, covering hundreds of thousands of acres with houses that were for the most part more pitiably devoid of architectural "style" than had been those of the 1920s "boom"); while on the other hand the Johnson Administration Building bears only upon the managerial and "white-collar" aspects of the industrial scene, thus leaving out of account the areas of human experience and of human concern where deep conflicts and tensions were being generated. Because of these limitations, together with its lack of an historical dimension and a genuinely political dimension, Wright's architecture falls short of making manifest that "system of philosophy and ethics" he said we had the right to expect from an architect.

Past and Future

A SECOND objection I would raise concerns Wright's relationship to Judeo-Christian eschatology. Is not his Broadacre scheme, and therewith his whole philosophical perspective, a mutilation of the very tradition out of which it is sprung—a secularization of a Biblical view of history and of ultimate salvation, even as were the progressivistic utopias of Proudhon, Comte, and Marx? Judging by the tone and substance of most of what Wright had to say about his brave new city, we would have to answer in the affirmative. His assertion that mechanization and electrification will inevitably usher in the streamlined millennium he envisioned is of the same order as Comte's declaration, a hundred years earlier, that serious warfare among advanced nations was no longer possible. Although both men formulated their ideas on the basis of Biblical thought, neither could fully accept the Biblical view of man's nature.

"Seventeenth century Protestants," writes H. Richard Niebuhr, "could not be utopians . . . for they did not share the fundamental presuppositions of utopianism—the beliefs that human ills are due to bad institutions, that a fresh start with good institutions will result in a perfect commonwealth, and that human reason is sufficiently wise, or human will sufficiently selfless, to make the erection of a perfect society possible." [8] Wright's thought stems not from Reformation orthodoxy but from the rationalistic progressivism of the eighteenth century. His vision of Broadacre City is prefigured in the glowing image of the practical paradise which was traced by Jonathan Edwards' disciple Samuel Hopkins (1721-1803), who foresaw a time when all men would have "sufficient leisure to pursue and acquire learning of every kind that will be beneficial to themselves and to society; great advances will be made in all arts and sciences and in every useful branch of knowledge, which tends to promote the spiritual and eternal good of men, or their convenience and comfort in this life," and so on.[9] What Wright pictures for us is akin to the paradisiacal garden of the Ghent Altarpiece: we are invited to behold "a flowered meadow beside the stream . . . bordered with ranks of trees, tiers gradually rising in height above the flowers at ground level," [10] and beyond the meadow a scattering of varied and noble towers shimmering in the sunlight. But instead of prophets and martyrs we find superhighways and traffic interchanges; instead of pilgrim saints and just judges, angeloid helicopters and jet-propelled trains; and there is no Lamb, no mystic adoration.

Speaking of Marxism, Löwith says, "The Communist creed, though a pseudo-morphosis of Jewish-Christian messianism, lacks the fundamentals of it: the free acceptance of humiliation and of redemptive suffering as the condition of triumph. The proletarian Communist wants the crown without the cross; he wants to triumph by earthly happiness." [11] Much the same can be said of Wright, who asks us voluntarily to demolish the existing world, with all its evidences of history and of human insufficiency, and to build in its place a timeless new city which will provide us with all the comforts and conveniences our inventive engineers can conceive of—fast cars, trains, and planes, smoke-free air, well-built houses, air-conditioned factories, ubiquitous laboratories, good management. But is this not in all truth a degraded image of the New Earth—an unspeakable corruption of what St. John and the Van Eycks had in mind?

8. H. Richard Niebuhr, *The Kingdom of God in America* (Hamden, Conn.: The Shoe String Press, 1956; first published in 1935), p. 49.
9. *Ibid.*, pp. 145-46.
10. "Broadacre City: a New Community Plan," p. 249.
11. Karl Löwith, *Meaning in History* (Chicago: University of Chicago Press, 1949), p. 46.

Though there may be truth in the charge, two things must be said by way of qualification. In the first place, Broadacres is not an exercise in science fiction; Wright does not proffer technological marvels as sources of paradisiacal joy. Unlike the scientophile, he sees no goodness in scientific advancement *per se*. Goodness and joy lie where they have always lain—in the experience of freedom, of work, of fellowship, of the life of the family and the beauties of nature; and science can have no purpose other than to facilitate or promote these experiences. Having worked on his uncle's farm, Wright well knew the back-breaking laboriousness of life in the country and fully appreciated the power of the machine to lighten that burden; wherefore Broadacre City is fully mechanized. But he did not imagine that goodness lay in sheer abundance or in a perpetual escalation of the standard of living, especially if they are to be had at the cost of a man's freedom or of his participation with others in satisfying and meaningful work.

It would appear that the country has now decided to give science its head, to take us wheresoever it will, regardless of cost. But as it has rushed forward in the twentieth century, art has become drained of high meaning, music has floundered, architecture has been sterilized. Perhaps we need to be reminded that the sources of joy have not changed, that no new sources have been discovered in the laboratory or the technological center. Broadacres is such a reminder.

And secondly, for all his show of progressivistic optimism, Wright recognized the inaccessibility of Broadacres. He liked to proclaim that his plan was a real, even an inescapable, solution to all our difficulties; but on at least one occasion he was constrained to admit that we cannot build Broadacre City, and that even if it existed we should not be fit to enter. In the course of the dialogue with which *Architecture and Modern Life* concludes, Wright is brought around to saying, "I don't think Broadacre City would be fit for humans that have been more or less degraded by the circumstances in which they now live. Something would have to be done for them while they last. Some preparation for their end." [12] But since all of us, including Wright himself, have been so degraded by the world, it follows that there are no candidates for

12. *Architecture and Modern Life,* p. 328.

admission. Because of our corruption, we cannot build Broadacres with our own hands, any more than can the sinner, according to Christian and especially Protestant belief, save himself by his own efforts. Broadacres is whole and complete—"everywhere or nowhere," as Wright repeatedly insisted. It is without past or future. It lies outside history altogether, and no descendant of Adam, thrust into depravity simply by being born into the world of history, is worthy of entering. In the very last analysis Wright was compelled to recognize the reality of that aspect of the human condition that Calvin called original sin.

The ultimate mission of Organic Architecture, as Wright saw it, was to achieve the universal salvation of mankind; yet he understood that the mission could not be accomplished in the world as it stands. Granting the unattainability of paradise, however, something must be done for men "while they last. Some preparation for their end." One may describe the mission of the church in the same words. It is powerless to install the kingdom of God here and now, but it undertakes to ease men's burdens and to make "some preparation for their end." While accommodating itself to the world, it nevertheless attempts to uphold a standard by which the world must be judged and found wanting. So, too, with Wright's architecture: it speaks to the city and yet is not of the city; it is addressed to the American nation and is rooted in the nation's past, yet it stands against most of the values that are exemplified in the life of the nation. It accommodates itself to modern industrialism, but only for the sake of regaining, ultimately, an idyllic agrarianism, a perfect harmony between man and nature, that may be thought of as lying at either of the limits of history, the past or the future.

The industrialization and urbanization we have espoused and promoted have brought us into a world that has shown itself to be the easy prey of the specter of meaninglessness, on the one hand, and of new political absolutisms, on the other—as Proudhon and Burckhardt foresaw all too clearly more than a century ago. "Without a transcendent urge which outweighs all the clamor for power and money," wrote the latter, "nothing will be of any use." Wright's architecture declares the necessity of our preserving certain conceptions of goodness, of our reaffirming the validity of certain ideas about the nature of man and of his relation to the world. It is designed for the man who, as a single person with a proper name, knows himself to stand responsibily at the center of things. It is shaped by a "transcendent urge" that has more to do with Isaiah and Rousseau than with any aspect of what is commonly thought of as modern art.

For this reason it is often dismissed today as an anachronism, a latter-day exercise in Romanticism that is wholly irrelevant to the needs of the modern world. Anachronistic it unquestionably is; but one could make no more egregious error than to think that its relevancy would have been greater at some other time. What the Kaufmann house declares about the family would have been as much at odds with the conventional domesticity of the Victorian or any earlier era as it is with the domestic implications of the curtain-walled apartment monolith. What the Johnson building has to say about men's working together constitutes as devastating a judgment against the cruel industrialism of the 1830s as it does against the corporate giantism of the 1930s. Indeed, it is in the nature of all ideals that they claim for themselves a validity that is independent of the conditioning circumstances of a specific time or place. The Johnson building may have been pertinent to a situation in Wisconsin in 1936, but Wright would have contended that its truth depended not upon its pertinency but upon the very nature of man and his universal need to collaborate with his fellow beings. It may well be that Wright does not offer us an architectural style that we can use in our cities today—not, however, for the reason that it is irrelevant to our needs or to our situation, but rather because (1) it is based upon an inadequate and unduly sanguine interpretation of the ethical tradition it undertakes to defend, and (2) it advances an ideal that is incommensurate with the one on which the government of the country is based . . . though not so incommensurate as is the technologism of current architectural practice.

There are many indications in art today that we are teetering on the brink of a dark age. Landscape, portraiture, the *contrapposto* figure, narrative and dramatic subject matter, the perspective stagespace, the interplay of light and shadow—all these elements that are related to the centrality of the ethically responsible man have lately disappeared from painting, even as happened in the fifth century; while at the same time there has developed, as was the case in that earlier dark age, a taste for flattening, for geometrical patternization, and for motifs derived from primitive sources—or "barbarian," as they were once called. While goodness may ultimately emerge out of all this, the immediate prospect is not encouraging. Surely it were not inappropriate at this point to praise Wright for having taken his stand in defense of some of the oldest and best ideas of civilized man.

SHORT BIBLIOGRAPHY

WORKS BY WRIGHT:

An Autobiography, New York: Duell, Sloan & Pearce, 1943

Buildings, Plans, & Designs (Reprinting of Wasmuth monograph of 1910), New York: Horizon Press, 1943

Frank Lloyd Wright on Architecture: Selected Writings, 1894-1940, edited by Frederick Gutheim, New York: Duell, Sloan & Pearce, 1941

The Future of Architecture, New York: Horizon Press, 1953

Genius and Mobocracy, New York, Sloan & Pearce, 1949

The Living City, New York: Horizon Press, 1958

The Natural House, New York: Horizon Press, 1954

A Testament, New York: Horizon Press, 1957

Writings and Buildings, selected by Edgar Kaufmann & Ben Raeburn, New York: Meridian Books, 1960

WORKS ABOUT WRIGHT:

H. Allen Brooks, *The Prairie School*, Toronto: Univ. of Toronto Press, 1972

Finis Farr, *Frank Lloyd Wright, a Biography*, New York: Scribners, 1961

Henry-Russell Hitchcock, *In the Nature of Materials*, New York: Duell, Sloan & Pearce, 1942

Grant C. Manson, *Frank Lloyd Wright to 1910, the First Golden Age*, New York: Reinhold, 1958

Robert Twombly, *Frank Lloyd Wright, an Interpretive Biography*, New York: Harper & Row, 1973

John Lloyd Wright, *My Father Who Is on Earth*, New York: G. Putnam's Sons, 1946

INDEX